THE ULTIMATE
BRAZIL JIU-JITSU

Edited by Sarah Dzida, Raymond Horwitz, Edward Pollard,
Jeannine Santiago and Jon Sattler

Graphic design by John Bodine

Archival assistance and proofreading by Monique Perdue

©2008 Black Belt Communications LLC

All Rights Reserved
Printed in the United States of America
Library of Congress Control Number: 2008942249
ISBN-10: 0-89750-171-3
ISBN-13: 978-0-89750-171-2

First Printing 2008

WARNING

This book is presented only as a means of preserving a unique aspect of the heritage of the martial arts. Neither Ohara Publications nor the author make any representation, warranty or guarantee that the techniques described or illustrated in this book will be safe or effective in any self-defense situation or otherwise. You may be injured if you apply or train in the techniques illustrated in this book and neither Ohara Publications nor the author is responsible for any such injury that may result. It is essential that you consult a physician regarding whether or not to attempt any technique described in this book. Specific self-defense responses illustrated in this book may not be justified in any particular situation in view of all of the circumstances or under applicable federal, state or local law. Neither Ohara Publications nor the author make any representation or warranty regarding the legality or appropriateness of any technique mentioned in this book.

FOREWORD

In terms of public awareness, the world of martial arts is a fairly insular community, despite its international scope and broad influence. Outside the circle of dedicated students and fans of some notable competitor, it probably never really amounts to much on the radar screen of public opinion. Until recently, if you asked anyone on the street to name a famous martial artist, odds are they would say Bruce Lee. Younger people have probably heard about the tragic death of his son Brandon. And then what?

The answer is: Gracie. Even if this name stirs no recognition, it rings a bell. As this book is about to reveal, it is nearly impossible to consider the subject of mixed-martial arts fighting without first hearing about a member of the Gracie family. It could be because they are responsible for energizing and rejuvenating the practice of martial arts. It could be because word quickly spread about the 176-pound Royce Gracie defeating much larger men in open competitions.

Because the Gracie influence has become pandemic in martial arts, their particular discipline has come to be known as "Brazilian *jiu-jitsu*."

Here is the collected genesis of an emerging phenomenon as it was introduced in the pages of these magazines: *Black Belt*, *Martial Arts Training* and *Karate/Kung Fu Illustrated*. The contents have been carefully selected and arranged to provide both a useful guide and a fascinating picture of the incredible success curve that has made Brazilian jiu-jitsu the discipline and sport of a new era.

Edward Pollard
Black Belt Managing Editor

TABLE OF CONTENTS

GRACIE JIU-JITSU	8
GRACIE JIU-JITSU VS. THE WORLD	13
THE MAN WHO ACCEPTED THE GRACIE CHALLENGE	17
ROYCE GRACIE TAKES ALL COMERS IN THE UFC	21
THE BRAZILIAN JIU-JITSU INVASION	26
ROYCE GRACIE WINS UFC—AGAIN	35
HELIO GRACIE, THE FATHER OF BRAZILIAN JIU-JITSU	40
STILL KING OF THE HILL	43
ROYCE GRACIE'S CONDITIONING PROGRAM	50
TRAINING AT THE GRACIE ACADEMY	55
THE TWO-TIME UFC CHAMP IS ALL FOCUS	58
TEN REASONS WHY GRACIE JIU-JITSU WINS	61
ROYCE GRACIE SPEAKS	64
GRAPPLING IS LIKE SWIMMING	67
TOUGHEST MAN IN THE WORLD	69
IS RICKSON GRACIE THE ULTIMATE FIGHTER?	77
ROYCE ON OVERTRAINING	81
STREET JIU-JITSU VS. SPORT JIU-JITSU	85
WHO'S WHO IN GRACIE JIU-JITSU?	88
MODIFYING BRAZILIAN JIU-JITSU FOR VALE TUDO	93
IMPROVING THE IMAGE OF THE ART	101
JIU-JITSU TRAINING IN BRAZIL	103

ULTIMATE WARRIOR	108
THE TREASURE KEEPER	119
ATTACKS AND TRAPS FROM THE GUARD	125
SURVIVAL SPORT FOR WOMEN	129
PROVING GROUND	133
GRACIES IN ACTION	139
THE HOUSE THAT GRACIE BUILT	144
GRACIE UPDATE	149
THE MAN WHO CHANGED THE WORLD	156
UP CLOSE AND PERSONAL WITH KYRA GRACIE	165

GRACIE JIU-JITSU

by Don Beu • Photos by Rick Hustead • Black Belt • August 1989

Written accounts about Rorion Gracie can be misleading. Stories of how he tied up a roomful of Chuck Norris' black belts, or how he choked out kickboxer Ralph Algeria in less than three minutes, or how Navy SEALs come to him to hone their hand-to-hand combat skills can give you a mental picture of, well, Rambo.

Consequently, meeting Gracie is a bit of a jolt when you expect Rambo and are instead greeted with a warm smile and handshake by a man who, at least in terms of personality and education, has more in common with Gandhi.

Easygoing and articulate, Gracie could give diplomats lessons in charm and tact. And if his friendly, personable manner runs contrary to the distant, stoic manner we've come to expect from many Asian masters of the fighting arts, or the tough-talking bravado often shown by many American fighters and competitors, that's not unusual. This is because Gracie and his family have been challenging and defeating a lot of traditions and beliefs for more than six decades in their quest to prove the effectiveness of the martial art.

And while the Gracie clan is renowned for challenging and defeating fighters of virtually every style, behind the public victories are teaching and training methods that also challenge many traditional beliefs. This departure from tradition begins at the Gracie student's first class. For the average judo or *jujutsu* student, as well as students of other martial arts, the bulk of the first lesson is usually devoted to learning to fall safely. And the student's time with the instructor must often be shared with the rest of the class, usually also beginners who need the teacher's attention.

By contrast, the Gracie *jiu-jitsu* student's first lesson is a private one, as are the next 35 lessons of the basic course. In that first class, the student will learn five simple and effective techniques: escapes from a head lock, collar grab, front choke, bear hug and one ground-fighting technique.

Rather than spending at least half the class having the techniques practiced on him, the Gracie student spends the entire class practicing the techniques on the instructor, who provides constant feedback while the student perfects the moves through repetition.

And what about learning to fall? The student doesn't learn that until the 36th and final basic lesson. And while this flies in the face of conventional wisdom and may raise more than a few eyebrows among those concerned about safety, it's important to remember that the Gracie student is not being

THE ULTIMATE GUIDE TO BRAZILIAN JIU-JITSU

Rorion Gracie (standing)

thrown in practice. "In our system, the instructor takes the punishment," says Rorion, who believes it's more important that the student learn to fight effectively than to "take it."

While the average judo or jujutsu student goes home from his first class with his hands tingling from an hour or more spent slapping the mat during falling practice, the Gracie student goes home having practiced on five practical and effective self-defense techniques to the point at which they are almost a reflex. In the next class, those techniques will be reviewed and a few new ones will be shown. Every time the student comes to class, he will review the previous techniques and learn new ones. This constant repetition is what makes the techniques become reflexive.

Just as the Gracie approach to beginners departs from tradition, so does their approach to conditioning. No less an authority on grappling than Gene LeBell has said that being in shape is "more than half the battle" when it comes to being an effective fighter. For most martial artists, being in shape involves not just countless sit-ups, push-ups and jumping jacks but also plenty of running, skipping rope and frequent visits to the weight room.

"We don't like to do a lot of running," Gracie says. "We have some specific exercises for jiu-jitsu, but these involve mostly stretching for what I like to call 'combative flexibility,' like a cat."

One reason behind this laid-back outlook on conditioning lies in the overall philosophy of Gracie jiu-jitsu: simple techniques. A technique that requires a lot of skill or effort to apply is not practical against a bigger or stronger opponent, according to Gracie. "If you do it right, you don't have to do it fast," he says. If a martial artist takes the time to correctly apply an effective technique, Gracie says, winning a fight will take very little effort.

No better illustration of this can be seen than in the Gracies' success in the grueling arena of international-class *sambo*. Those familiar with the grappling arts would agree that sambo is a tough test of a fighter's endurance. But at the 1980 Pan American Sambo Championship, Gracie's brother Rickson beat several more extensively trained wrestlers and *judoka* to win the gold medal at 74 kilograms, while brothers Carlos and Rolls captured the silver and bronze medals at 80 and 68 kilograms, respectively.

As for the techniques themselves, they are amazingly effective and differ quite a bit from those found in conventional judo or jujutsu. A simple standing choke hold from the Gracie system, although similar in many ways to judo's *jui-jime* (cross choke), is actually more efficient. The difference between jui-jime and the Gracie standing choke hold is like the difference between stepping on the gas of a Volkswagen and a Porsche. The Gracie choke hold gets the job done a lot faster, and with a lot less effort.

Another thing missing from Gracie jiu-jitsu is adherence to Oriental etiquette and traditions. For example, in Gracie jiu-jitsu, nobody bows. "That's a part of Japanese culture," Rorion Gracie says. "I don't teach Japanese culture; I teach Gracie jiu-jitsu, which is from Brazil. A simple handshake is good enough for me."

Gracie claims this departure from tradition helps new students gain self-confidence and be more comfortable. "A student doesn't need to feel we're above him or anything," Gracie says. "We're not on top then, he feels on top. He's at home here. We're not gods that anybody needs to bow to; we're just a bunch of guys from Brazil."

Rather than concentrating on the nuances of rhythm, balance and timing, the Gracies spend a lot of time practicing situations that might occur in a street fight. New or revised techniques are constantly being added to the system. "This increases the gap between us and Japanese jujutsu, as well as other martial arts," Gracie says. "Gracie jiu-jitsu is for the person who is slow, weak or thinks he's not too intelligent. You don't have to be strong to do Gracie jiu-jitsu because the techniques are based on leverage. And you don't have to be smart because we drill on the techniques until they become a reflex."

Rorion Gracie (top)

Proof of the system's usefulness to slower, weaker individuals can be seen in a program Gracie has initiated at several Torrance, California, schools. Gracie and school counselors target kids who are having problems or are labeled "wimps" by their peers, and they introduce them to Gracie jiu-jitsu in an effort to instill them with self-confidence and self-esteem. "After just two classes, psychologists say one of the kids is a completely different person," Gracie claims.

It's significant that the same techniques that have helped to inspire confidence and maturity in troubled youngsters are also sought out for their effectiveness by groups with more pragmatic goals in mind, like the U.S. Navy SEALs and the Los Angeles County Sheriff's Department. Members of the SEALs have asked Gracie to work out a program for them. The SEALs like his techniques "because if they sneak up on a sentry and start punching the guy, pretty soon the whole country's going to know about it," Gracie asserts. "With our techniques, they can take care of things quietly."

Law-enforcement officials like the Gracie techniques because they can subdue and restrain suspects without violence. "It's more practical," Gracie says, "and it saves money in lawsuits."

Gracie would also like to demonstrate the effectiveness of his family's art against world heavyweight-boxing champion Mike Tyson. "We believe Tyson is unbeatable within the rules of boxing," Gracie notes, "but in a street fight against Gracie jiu-jitsu, we don't believe in Mike Tyson."

Gracie has been trying to arrange a fight, no holds barred, between his brother Rickson and Tyson for some time. But, perhaps remembering how unsuccessful past champions like Muhammad Ali have been against grapplers, Tyson has so far been uninterested.

Gracie jiu-jitsu succeeds in virtually all areas of the martial arts: competition (judo and sambo), police and military work, self-defense, and in building maturity and self-esteem in youth. Few, if any, other martial arts can claim to accomplish so much with the same basic training program and techniques. Fewer still are willing to back up their claims by taking on and defeating anyone who wants to test their skills. And even rarer are those who can do what Rorion Gracie can do: make friends in the process.

GRACIE JIU-JITSU VS. THE WORLD

by Clay McBride • Black Belt • September 1991

In an era when many martial artists go out of their way to avoid direct comparisons with rival stylists, the Gracie brothers cheerfully invite doubting individuals to test the combat worthiness of Gracie *jiu-jitsu* for themselves.

The Gracies' attitude goes against the popular conception that "it is the fighter, not the style" that determines the outcome of a confrontation. While acknowledging that individuals do exhibit different skill levels, the Gracies refuse to embrace the "all styles are equal" philosophy. They are polite but adamant in their insistence that Gracie jiu-jitsu is the most realistic, practical, empty-hand fighting art in the world.

These Brazilian jiu-jitsu stylists have further stirred the embers of controversy by issuing their famous open challenge: They are willing to prove the superiority of their art in "street-condition matches" against any opponent, of any style, at any time.

Clearly, Gracie jiu-jitsu is a devastating art. But how do you account for its effectiveness? And how are the Gracies able to transmit the essence of their style to their students so quickly? An examination of the concepts and teaching methods employed by the Gracies provides the answers.

Concepts

According to Rorion Gracie, the value of a martial art is not predicated solely on the skills of its practitioners. The art itself possesses specific qualities that can be used to gauge its effectiveness.

Simply singling out individual techniques, however, tells you little about an art. The effectiveness of a style does not lie in isolated movements. To appreciate the sophistication and practicality of a given approach, you must probe the framework in which the techniques are used—the concepts behind the application.

The Gracies contend that their art is superior to other styles, and a cursory examination of their jiu-jitsu system would seem to reveal several strategic advantages. The following are three of those advantages:

Windows and margins—In the real world, opponents seldom fight with the synchronized grace one observes in sparring sessions between classmates. Men intent on inflicting damage clash with unexpected suddenness. They shift position constantly, refusing to maintain a specific range, and move in wildly unpredictable patterns and broken rhythms.

Punch and kick practitioners, conversely, work within a specific range of combat. Their "window of opportunity" is very small. If their strike falls short of its target by as little as an inch, it is relatively ineffective. If it lands prematurely, its power may be reduced by as much as 80 percent. Facing an opponent who refuses to maintain a uniform distance, a punch/kick stylist will find it difficult to deliver lethal blows. His dependency on pinpoint precision leaves him with a narrow margin for error.

The Gracie jiu-jitsu practitioner has no trouble maintaining his chosen range. He simply holds on. Timing his entry, the Gracie fighter either catches his opponent in a moment of overextension or jams his enemy, smothering his technique. Once the entry has been safely accomplished, the Gracie student secures his hold. There is no need for pinpoint accuracy; any solid grip will work nicely. Within moments, the Gracie stylist executes a takedown, putting his opponent on the ground. From this position, the Gracie fighter's window of opportunity is unlimited. With his foe held indefinitely at the ideal range, the Gracie practitioner can attempt any number of techniques in rapid succession. His margin for error is enlarged because his enemy is locked in the perfect position, allowing the Gracie stylist the time to apply his techniques for maximum effect.

Transitions—Martial arts magazines often depict punch/kick practitioners blocking an opponent's attack and then scoring with a series of blows. The punch/kick artist's retaliation is usually uninterrupted by the attacker, who stands cooperatively, his initial punch still hanging in space. The illusion created is one of flawless transition on the part of the martial artist. His techniques flow smoothly, one into the next, unimpeded by his frozen opponent.

These "technique-in-a-vacuum" displays, while pleasing to the eye, are misleading. In a real confrontation, the attacker is shifting, dodging and twisting. He is flailing with unorthodox yet powerful punches and kicks; he doesn't just stand by and wait to get hit.

The key to a successful style lies not only in striking techniques but also in the transitions between techniques. Many striking arts do not provide the student with the necessary movements to allow him to neutralize his enemy's aggressions while mounting his own counteroffensive. Any scenario in which an opponent is allowed to move freely while exchanging blows is fraught with peril. It is simple mathematics: The more chances an opponent has to swing, the greater the probability he will connect.

In Gracie jiu-jitsu, there is a saying: First you survive, then you win. To put it another way: Neutralize your attacker's aggression, then apply your offensive techniques. The Gracie fighter neutralizes his opponent's arms and legs, smothering his technique. Applying simple takedowns, the Gracie stylist robs his enemy of his balance and thus his power. Once on the ground, the Gracie practitioner controls his opponent's every movement, manipulating him into a vulnerable position for a finishing technique. As the Gracie stylist maneuvers his enemy toward defeat, he constantly checks any retaliation, neutralizing counterattacks before they develop. By restricting his opponent's movement, he limits his enemy's ability to injure him.

The familiarization factor—When a punch/ kick stylist spars with a partner in class, he maintains a mutually agreed on distance, one naturally suited for punching and kicking. Exchanging techniques at this specific range, he is lulled into a sense of false security, believing his defensive skills are sufficiently honed to repel an attacker determined to grab him. If by some implausible fluke he did end up on the ground, he believes his eye jabs, groin punches or throat strikes will humble and subdue any foolish "rassler." Of course, the punch/kick artist has never tested any of these beliefs in anything approximating actual conditions. He just knows he is right. Why should he bother to familiarize himself with a style of fighting that poses no real threat? Countless practitioners have passed sweetly into unconsciousness asking themselves that very question.

Unlike the punch/kick stylist, the Gracie student has spent a great deal of time studying the techniques and tactics of his enemy. He respects the tools at his opponent's disposal, but he also knows how to exploit the weaknesses of different styles because he has matched his grappling skills against them. According to the old adage, when two opponents of equal skill and strength meet, the more seasoned man will win. When it comes to combat, the Gracie jiu-jitsu stylist is the more seasoned man.

Teaching

It is one thing for a martial artist to possess outstanding skills. It is quite another for him to be able to convey those skills to someone else. The best martial artist does not always make the best teacher. Fortunately for their students, the Gracie brothers also excel as educators. Their teaching principles, like their art, are simple, direct and effective for the following reasons:

One-on-one instruction—While a student may later choose to participate in a group class, his first 36 lessons in Gracie jiu-jitsu are private. There are no distractions, no idle time. The student has the undivided attention of his teacher for the entire class. Under such intense scrutiny, the student's strengths and weaknesses are quickly revealed. The instructor soon familiarizes himself with his student's nature and psychology, finding the best ways to motivate and challenge the pupil.

Learning by doing—In Gracie jiu-jitsu training, the word "hypothetical" does not exist. There are no choreographed exchanges of attack and defense, no step-by-step rehearsals of "appropriate responses" to possible situations, no one-step sparring. From the moment you step onto the mat until the moment class ends, you are executing throws, takedowns, chokes, arm and leg locks, holds, escapes, reversals, etc. Each technique flows into the next, the specific order dictated only by the moment-to-moment reality of the match. This dizzying stream of moves pauses only when a student reaches a predicament for which he has no response. At that point, the instructor provides another tiny piece of the puzzle and the *randori* (free exercise) continues. Hundreds of movements are compressed into each class, all of them performed in a continuous chain.

Another distinct advantage to learning Gracie jiu-jitsu involves the nature of the techniques themselves. Choking and joint-locking maneuvers are an inherently more humane way to subdue an attacker than smashing his head or ribs. Jiu-jitsu techniques allow students to practice levels of power and intensity; they do not have to "pull" their techniques. They can apply increasing pressure until the opponent submits.

Gradually, the pupil is allowed to grapple with fellow practitioners while the teacher supervises. Often this occurs at the end of a student's class, when he is fatigued. Robbed of his strength and endurance, the student must rely on technique to overcome his fresh opponent.

Teaching by example—If a student questions what it means to be a good martial artist, he need look no further than the Gracie brothers. They are committed to seeing that their students learn properly and completely the art of Gracie jiu-jitsu. They teach with great affection. They do not criticize, they encourage. They do not ridicule, they inspire. Instead of frustration, they offer challenge.

And that's a Gracie challenge everyone can endorse.

THE MAN WHO ACCEPTED THE GRACIE CHALLENGE
by Scot Conway • Photo by Rick Hustead • Black Belt • April 1992

Most people in the martial arts community are familiar by now with the Gracie *jiu-jitsu* challenge: The Gracie brothers have offered to take on all comers to demonstrate the effectiveness of their Brazilian jiu-jitsu. Rorion Gracie, the head instructor at the Gracie Jiu-Jitsu Academy, notes that the challenge has been open for more than half a century and that Gracie jiu-jitsu stands virtually undefeated. The terms of engagement are simple: one on one, no weapons, no eye gouges and no groin strikes. There is some latitude for negotiation, as long as the adjustments in terms are reasonable.

As a former student of *kara-ho kempo* instructor Sam Kuoha, I was satisfied with the street effectiveness of kempo karate, yet I wondered how my style would stack up against a skilled grappler. One thing about grapplers: If they are really good, you have no choice but to play their game. Most punches and all kicks require a certain amount of space to execute properly. If a grappler successfully closes the distance and starts wrestling with you, an arsenal of punches and kicks is suddenly useless. A good combat grappler simply will not leave himself open for striking maneuvers.

Although a black belt in kempo, I knew my grappling skills were marginal. I wanted to learn more on the subject, and what better way to do so than to accept the Gracie challenge?

My intent was not to beat the Gracies; after all, if no one else had defeated them in 50-plus years, I shouldn't expect to be the first. I simply wanted to learn more about their style. I didn't want theory, I wanted application. I didn't want competition jiu-jitsu, I wanted street grappling. And I thought the best way to get such information was to fight a grappler. And if you're going to fight a grappler, why not fight the best? So I telephoned the Gracie Jiu-Jitsu Academy to set up a match, and they accepted.

Many people have leveled criticism at the Gracies, calling their challenge arrogant, but in the conversations leading up to my scheduled contest, Rorion was always courteous and polite. He had the tone of a man who was very confident. Some might interpret his manner as condescending, but when you're undefeated, confidence can come across that way. He was always very respectful, and very businesslike. Rorion impressed me as a man who was concerned about the self-defense quality of martial arts. Both of us believed that many self-defense applications taught in martial arts schools today are just theory and all too often fail when the student needs them the most.

The day of the match soon rolled around and I, along with two of my students, drove up from San Diego to the academy in Torrance, California. I would not be facing Rorion but his 25-year-old brother Royler, who was 5 feet 9 inches tall, weighed 140 pounds, was a third-degree black belt in jiu-jitsu and was "born on the mat," according to Rorion. I was also 5 feet 9 inches tall, but I was only a first-degree black belt and gave away several years in experience to my adversary. But I weighed in at 165 pounds—25 more than Royler, so I was still enthusiastic as I stepped out on the mat and the fight began.

Royler made the first move, but I didn't respond immediately. I waited until the moment I thought I would have had the legal right of self-defense if the bout had taken place on the street. By then, it was too late. Royler got on my back, locked himself in and started pummeling me. I managed a groin grab, but anyone with street-fighting experience knows that adrenaline will allow a fighter to ignore the effects of such a damaging move until after the bout. The pain the opponent experiences can even become a motivating force, driving the attacker on to even greater violence.

I tried to find a way out of the hold but found that my grappling skills were not up to the task. Royler, meanwhile, continued to pummel my head. He could not hit especially hard while maintaining his grip, and I thought I could probably take several minutes of the pounding before slipping into unconsciousness. But because Royler had me in a hold, he could take as long as he needed. So I called the fight and gave round one to Gracie jiu-jitsu.

As my students tended to my injuries, I had time to reflect on the bout. My conclusion: You can't wait long to counter if your opponent knows how to grapple.

After a few minutes, I decided to have another go at it. Realizing that I wouldn't be able to escape once Royler had me in a good hold, I decided I would call the second fight if and when a hold was locked in.

This time, I took a slightly more aggressive posture and tried to fend off Royler's advance with a low side kick. It worked ... for about half a second. Royler moved in just as I re-chambered the leg and, before I could throw another technique, I was grabbed again. This time, however, I managed to catch Royler in a more vulnerable position, and my heel struck him hard twice on the back. I attempted a scissor lock, but Royler escaped and once again climbed on my back. I took one hit and called the bout. Royler was visibly upset, but he honored the terms of the contest and halted his attack. Game, set and match to Gracie jiu-jitsu.

Both bouts were very short: The first lasted 45 seconds, and the second was over in half a minute. If they had been real fights and had been al-

THE ULTIMATE GUIDE TO BRAZILIAN JIU-JITSU

Rorion Gracie

lowed to reach a natural conclusion, I almost certainly would have been pummeled into unconsciousness; Royler had me at his mercy.

Weeks later, I was still wondering if I had taken the right approach to the match. After all, there were a number of techniques in my kempo arsenal that I had never considered using: joint- and neck-breaking maneuvers, groin smashes, and a host of other potentially debilitating moves. The problem is, how can you justify severely injuring someone who is just wrestling with you? If such dangerous techniques had been successfully applied, I would likely be sitting in a California prison, serving time for aggravated assault. Deep down, I do not really believe that many of the aforementioned techniques could have been successfully applied against Royler. While some options do appear available to me on the videotape of the match, the dynamics of the actual fight prevented them.

I came to several conclusions after the match. First, you can't rely on striking techniques against a good grappler—not if you intend to fight within the bounds of the law. Second, if you wait until a grappler has done enough to warrant the legal use of self-defense, it will probably be too late to strike back effectively. And third, if you hope to legally defeat a grappler, you had better be skilled in the art of grappling.

Many in the martial arts community speak of what they would do if pitted against the Gracie brothers. Most of these individuals generally claim superiority over the Gracie technique—and perhaps they could defeat the Gracies in a match. But until they have actually stepped onto the mat with one of the Gracies and proven their point, it's all simply idle chatter. For one-on-one fighting without weapons, I discovered that Gracie jiu-jitsu is tough to beat.

I will forever be remembered as a man who once fought Royler Gracie and lost. But what I won was far more important. I won knowledge, experience and insight. And for a martial arts instructor, that is victory enough.

ROYCE GRACIE TAKES ALL COMERS IN THE UFC

by Robert W. Young • Photo by Rick Hustead • Karate/Kung Fu Illustrated • April 1994

When the smoke had cleared after the Ultimate Fighting Championship in Denver, the man who triumphed was Royce Gracie. In the very brief process of eliminating his three opponents on the way to final victory, the 6-foot-l-inch, 176-pound native of Rio de Janeiro, Brazil, avoided all injury except for a nip on the ear. In fact, Gracie dispatched a boxer, shootwrestler and *savate* practitioner without even breaking a sweat.

Yet this monumental victory over such varied fighters has not given the Torrance, California-based *jiu-jitsu* instructor, who could rightly be called the toughest fighter in America, a big head or an arrogant attitude. He insists that the UFC has not changed him or altered his plans for the future. Royce Gracie, along with older brother Rorion, will continue teaching his family's martial art in Southern California, as he has done for the past seven years.

"I am 27 years old, and I've been doing jiu-jitsu for 28 years," Gracie jokes. "I learned jiu-jitsu from my father, Helio Gracie, and my brothers. My dad and three brothers still teach in Brazil." After the UFC event, Gracie told a reporter he had fought not for the $50,000 prize but for the honor of his family, which issued the Gracie Challenge—an open invitation to take on any fighter under virtually any set of rules—in Brazil more than 65 years ago.

Even before the UFC started, Gracie knew he would win. "I had total confidence; there was no doubt," he says. "[The competitors were] very good at what they do; they are strong guys. Between them, it was a big struggle—you can see how they broke [each other's] noses. But I didn't think it was that much of a competition for me. My biggest opponent there was my mind."

Against the Boxer

In his first match, Gracie kept International Boxing Federation cruiserweight champion Art Jimmerson at bay with kicks to the knee area. "[My older brother] Rickson told me, 'With the boxer, just sit down and wait a little bit. There's no hurry coming in and getting ahold of him,'" Gracie says. "So I just circled around and waited a little to see what he was going to do."

"The boxer didn't want to [fight barehanded] because he didn't want to break his knuckles," Gracie says. "The gloves were to protect his hands, not my face. First he was going to fight with no gloves, then he decided to put gloves on because he didn't want to hurt his hands. But then he took one glove off. I think his plan was to punch hard with his right and break his hand on my face. And his jab would not be hurt."

Jimmerson never got a chance to punch Gracie because the jiu-jitsu stylist's takedown put the boxer on his back, with Gracie riding his chest. Jimmerson tapped out before Gracie could apply a finishing hold.

Against the Shootwrestler

One of the most interesting matches of the UFC pitted Patrick Smith, the 1993 Sabaki Challenge champion, against Ken Shamrock, a top-ranked shootwrestler. Both fighters ended up on the ground, and Smith struggled to get an ankle lock on Shamrock but couldn't. "He doesn't know how," Gracie says. "He was trying but didn't know what to do. It is easy when you know how to do it."

When his turn with Shamrock came, Gracie fought differently. Rickson advised him to change his strategy. "[He told me,] 'Don't wait and study him; don't even breathe. Just go, shoot in, take over,'" Gracie says. "So I just walked straight up to him and got in a clinch right away."

"The shootwrestler knew how to [apply a foot lock], and I knew how to do it, but I also knew how to escape," Gracie says. The match provided some excitement and a bit of suspense, until Gracie wound up on top. "He forgot to protect his neck," he says. "He tried to go for a foot lock, but he forgot that I would try to go for a choke." Shamrock tapped out seconds later.

Against the Savate Stylist

In the final fight, Gracie faced savate stylist Gerard Gordeau. Before the match, "Rickson just said, 'Do whatever you want. It's up to you now,'" Gracie says. He waited a little, then charged in for the takedown. After a brief struggle, during which the two fighters stood against the wire fence surrounding the ring, they fell to the mat.

The only injury Gracie sustained in the UFC occurred during a clinch when Gordeau bit his ear. "When we went to the ground and I got on top of him, he got a bite on my ear," Gracie says. "I pulled it out [of his mouth] and looked at him, and he looked at me like, 'So what?'"

Before the match, Gordeau and Gracie had agreed to prohibit biting and eye gouging. "That was cheating," Gracie says. "That's one thing that gets me upset. So I head-butted him a couple of times in the face." Less than two minutes into the fight, Gracie succeeded with his choke hold, and Gordeau tapped out.

Caliber of the Competitors

Before the UFC, some pundits predicted that the jiu-jitsu practitioner would win because only he has extensive experience fighting other stylists and he feels very comfortable on the ground. But Gracie disagrees: "The other guys probably got involved in street fights, and once you get involved in martial arts, you're always going to deal with somebody with a different style. I have experience with different styles, [but] they probably have their own experiences."

Gracie agrees that he is most comfortable fighting on the ground. "I'm not going to fight them standing up; I'm going to get my clinch and take them to the ground," he says. "It's like a shark—a shark is not going to fight you in the desert. He's going to bring you to the ocean."

Other complaints centered on the caliber of the competition. "Yes, the kickboxer was ... out of shape, but you [must remember] that he was the heavyweight champion two times," Gracie says. "Just because [the boxer] didn't do anything against me, it doesn't mean he is not the No. 8 cruiserweight in the IBF. The shootfighter [is] No. 1 in Japan; just because he lost in 57 seconds and it looked so easy doesn't mean the guy is nothing. They are champions in what they do."

After the UFC, amid broken hands, smashed noses, bleeding eyes and missing teeth, perhaps the most pressing question for martial artists was, Is it normal for a Gracie jiu-jitsu practitioner to win three fights and not get hit even once? "That's the idea," Gracie says. "I fought at about 176 [pounds], so I couldn't afford to get hit by those guys. I couldn't afford to get hit by Gerard Gordeau—he knocked [410-pound sumo competitor] Teila Tuli on his butt. You think he's not going to knock me out with one of his hits?"

Jiu-Jitsu for Everyone

The Gracie family does not teach students to react in certain ways against a grappler and in different ways against a boxer or a kicker. Gracie likens his family's system to cooking. "I'm going to teach you how to cook plain rice," he says. "You're the one who's going to say, 'Well, this guy deserves a little pepper.' And you hit him as much as you want. I'm not going to tell you to hit. I'm just going to teach you how to cook plain rice."

In each confrontation, the individual must decide to hit, wait or walk away. "I teach you how to take care of business," Gracie says. "If you want to be mean, that's up to you. If you want to run after him or run away from him, it's up to you."

Practitioners of other martial arts can easily pick up useful skills from

BLACK BELT

Royce Gracie (top)

this realistic style of jiu-jitsu without abandoning their art, Gracie says. "It will be much better if they can mix [their style and jiu-jitsu] together," he says. "You should always keep your mind open. There's nothing wrong with knowing how to hit or kick. There's nothing wrong with knowing how to take a guy down to the ground and choke him out."

The need for such offensive versatility was succinctly illustrated by Gordeau's match; a single punch to Tuli's head broke his hand, and a single kick to the sumo player's face cut his foot. "That's why you have to know how to do a little bit of each one, instead of just sticking with one thing," Gracie advises.

The Future of Martial Arts

Gracie believes his UFC victory will change martial arts in the United States. "It will open everybody's eyes—especially the weaker guys—that you don't have to be a monster to be the champ. You don't have to be the biggest guy or the one who hits the hardest. And you don't have to get hurt in a fight. When professional guys like that fight, [some think that, as one fighter said], 'You have to be able to take pain.' He [can] take the pain; I would rather apply the pain," Gracie says, laughing.

With 16 UFC events planned for the next five years, and the Bahamas, Puerto Rico, Denver and Japan vying for the rights to host the next one, martial artists around the world have much to look forward to. No doubt, many are wondering whether Gracie might compete against another jiu-jitsu stylist in the next UFC. "In jiu-jitsu, we are like a family, so it's hard for us to fight against each other," he says. "But what could happen is, somebody like Gerard Gordeau could learn some jiu-jitsu and then come fight me. But even if he wins, it's a credit to me because he's beating me with jiu-jitsu."

THE BRAZILIAN JIU-JITSU INVASION

by Steve Neklia and Robert W. Young • Photos by Rick Hustead • Karate/Kung Fu Illustrated • June 1994

Jiu-jitsu from Brazil has become one of the hottest martial arts in the United States. Few can argue that Royce Gracie's seemingly effortless grappling victory in the 1993 Ultimate Fighting Championship and his family's efforts to spread its brand of jiu-jitsu are not making a great impact on the world's martial arts community. Likewise, fans of Chuck Norris' *Walker, Texas Ranger* TV series have to admit how natural the action star looks when he finishes his adversaries using jiu-jitsu armbars and chokes he learned from the Machado brothers.

In 1981, the Gracie family took its fighting style out of its rough-and-tumble Brazilian birthplace and popularized it in the Western United States. But since then, Machado jiu-jitsu has sprung up in Southern California, and Brazilian jiu-jitsu has recently arrived in San Diego and on the East Coast. What follows is an investigative overview that will help introduce the Brazilian art form from the roots up.

Jiu-Jitsu by Gracie

George Gracie emigrated from Scotland in 1801 and settled in Brazil, Rorion Gracie says. Years later, George's grandson, Gastao Gracie, befriended Esai Maeda, also known as Count Koma, the chief of a Japanese immigration colony who was assigned to Brazil in 1914. In gratitude, Maeda, a former *jujutsu* champion in Japan, taught his martial art to Carlos Gracie, Gastao's son. In 1925, Carlos and his four brothers opened the first jujutsu school in Brazil. Carlos' brother, Helio Gracie, later developed new techniques, smoothed out the transitions between them and created the undefeated system the family now teaches. "The essence is [techniques] that don't require strength, speed or coordination," Rorion says.

Royce, Rorion's brother, recounts a key episode involving his uncle, Carlos, and his father, Helio: "My dad was a small guy; he was very weak. So my dad would sit all day long just watching my uncle teach. One day, my uncle was late for a class, so my dad started teaching. From that day on, [none of] the students ever took a class with my uncle again. They liked my dad's new way."

Although the Gracie style of jiu-jitsu derives its well-known effectiveness from Japanese jujutsu, its specialization in ground fighting differentiates it from other brands of the ancient grappling art. "This style of jiu-jitsu that we have, they are trying to hide so much in Japan—that's the story that

I heard—that it became judo, *aikido* and the [styles of] jujutsu they have around here," Royce says. "They hid so much that they forgot their own [art]. The style [we practice] doesn't exist in Japan anymore."

Other jujutsu schools teach mostly standing techniques intended to restrain an attacker. "We have lots of that; it's just that we're more [geared] toward the ground than they are," Royce says. "We have a lot of joint techniques, a lot of twisting here and there—like the normal jujutsu. It's just that they stick with that. We go to the ground and study [it] because a lot of fights end up there once you get in a clinch."

Rorion emphasizes that his family's claim to fame is Helio's new way of teaching streamlined jujutsu techniques, not the creation of a new art. He says the term "Gracie jiu-jitsu" is actually a misnomer: "My style is called jiu-jitsu; Gracie jiu-jitsu is not a style. We learned from a former Japanese

Rorion Gracie (top)

champion that went to Brazil, so we're teaching the traditional Japanese style. What makes our system unique is not that we have a different technique—my arm lock hurts as much an anybody else's. The difference is that we have the Gracie Challenge."

But if the Gracies claim their techniques are the same as those of other styles of jujutsu, why has the popularity of the art they teach skyrocketed? "We might have a different way of teaching," Rorion suggests. "Some people get involved in jiu-jitsu and like the South American friendship, the family, the attitude, the fact that we have self-confidence. But the techniques are the same as everybody else's. There's a growing controversy regarding the Gracie system—it's not the Gracie system; it's the Gracie personality. That's the difference. And we show that we have the responsibility toward our students to back up every technique we teach. That's the origin of the Gracie Challenge."

The Gracie Challenge went out to martial artists in Brazil more than 65 years ago. "We are willing to back up what we're saying. I'm willing to put my money where my mouth is," Rorion says. "Gracie representatives are ready to prove their effectiveness against fighters of all styles in a no-holds-barred event. We have not been defeated in 65 years." Rorion insists that the Gracie Challenge was not created to put down different martial arts or artists. "The only way to see what's really effective is to go to the mat," he says.

As the news of their victories spread throughout the martial arts community of Brazil, it bestowed on the Gracies a fame for street effectiveness most martial artists would envy. Obviously, the Gracie name has become a valuable commodity for those teaching jiu-jitsu, so much so that Rorion recently registered "Gracie Jiu-Jitsu" as an official service mark to prevent unauthorized usage.

The registration was necessary "because Gracie is my name, first of all," he says, "so I'm protecting my name. The trademark is not to separate the style; it's to protect [the name]. Gracie is the means to teach jiu-jitsu. I protected the name because Gracie represents effectiveness and the Gracie Challenge. Saying 'I teach the Gracie system' is a way for people to get linked to the Gracie Challenge and earn the respect and prestige ... we have developed over the years. [If they want], they can develop their own challenge and their own system and build their own name just like I did."

To cope with the growing numbers of people who want to study Brazilian jiu-jitsu under a certified Gracie instructor, the Gracie Jiu-Jitsu Academy has decided on a slow expansion. "We have three guys going through the instructor's program," Royce says. "They are not black belts yet, but we are teaching them how to teach, and they are helping us in class. Once they get good enough to go on their own, we might get another group of guys and [send them through the course]."

The only two certified representatives of the academy who do not belong to the Gracie family are Fabio Santos in Torrance, California, and Pedro Sauer in Provo, Utah, Rorion says. "Everybody else who claims to teach Brazilian jiu-jitsu, to have learned with the Gracies ... they're trying to take advantage and capitalize on the name," he says.

Yet the Gracie Jiu-Jitsu Academy in Los Angeles is not the only place students can learn jiu-jitsu from a Gracie. Rickson Gracie—the world open weight class jiu-jitsu champion who is featured prominently in the *Gracie Jiu-Jitsu in Action* videotape—teaches in Santa Monica, California. In the past, Rickson's students have competed against Royce's student in friendly competition. In Honolulu, jiu-jitsu instruction is available from Relson Gracie, another son of Helio who operates in conjunction with the Gracie Jiu-Jitsu Academy. And in Corona del Mar, California, Reylson Gracie, a son of Carlos who is not associated with the academy, teaches the grappling art.

Enter the Machados

Like their cousins, the Gracies, the Machado brothers—Carlos, Roger, Rigan, Jean Jacques and John—are another martial arts family from Brazil. They are third-generation practitioners of Brazilian jiu-jitsu and nephews of Carlos Gracie. "We learned from the late Rolls Gracie and later Carlos Gracie Jr. and Crolin Gracie, who are all Carlos Gracie's sons," Rigan says.

"When we were in Brazil, we were the top students from Carlos Gracie Jr.'s school," John adds, "and we defended his school against other schools until we came here." The brothers also taught at the academy and won a number of Brazilian jiu-jitsu, world jujutsu and *sambo* tournaments.

Carlos Machado says he, John and Rigan arrived in the United States in April 1990, and Jean Jacques and Roger followed. They began giving lessons in 1992. "We started teaching in our house, but we got too many students," John says. "Then we met Chuck Norris, and he helped us open our school in Encino, [California]. [We met him] through Richard Norton." Norton, a martial artist and action film star, has studied with the Machados for several years.

The Machados claim they left Brazil so their style of jiu-jitsu could grow. "We think that in America, we had a lot better chance to succeed," Carlos says. "We also wanted to be pioneers because what we are doing is a unique approach. We teach jiu-jitsu with the philosophical aspects; we want to make sure [martial arts and philosophy] go together. Our schools are like a home for the students; we help them in self-defense and many other areas of their lives."

"For us, jiu-jitsu is a way of life," John says. "We teach respect for family and other martial artists, mostly vegetarian nutrition—it becomes a way of life. That's how we learned it from our uncle, who is a famous nutritionist back home, and that's how we do it."

Rigan claims that the jiu-jitsu he and his brothers teach differs from what is taught in Brazil. "It's changed because, from the time Japanese jujutsu came to Brazil until today, three generations [have passed]—more than 60 years," he says. "Brazilian jiu-jitsu concentrates almost 80 percent on the ground. Japanese jujutsu concentrates on other points and not much on the ground."

"The Japanese had their [jujutsu] peak before judo became more popular," Carlos says. "When jujutsu became restricted, [instructors] were ostracized, and they didn't practice much. But in Brazil, we had fertile soil for that art, and our family developed it over the years. We still use a lot of techniques we inherited [from the Japanese], but we have added other things we discovered."

Of all the countries in the world, the Machados claim their super-effective style could have developed only in the Brazil of the past. "The cultural aspects of Brazil are very important," John says. "When our uncle, Carlos Gracie, started [teaching jujutsu] with his brothers, he met a lot of cultural resistance because people didn't want to accept a new style. In our Latin country, where we have the culture of being macho, they had to prove [its effectiveness] through fighting ... like the Ultimate Fighting Championship. He did that many, many times and [in matches] much tougher than that."

In the United States, the Machados promote their brand of jiu-jitsu not through inter-style challenge matches but through a spirit of cooperation. "Ninety percent of our students are from different martial arts," Carlos says. "When they come, we show them what we have. We don't question their background or experience and say whether that's good or bad, or whether it applies to grappling. We just show them [our style], and if they like it, they join our class and blend jiu-jitsu with what they already know."

Part of their promotional strategy has included developing relationships with famous American martial artists. "Chuck Norris, Gene LeBell, Benny Urquidez, Bob Wall—we try to open doors and make friends with all of them," Carlos says. Soon after Norris encountered the brothers' formidable jiu-jitsu skills, he incorporated part of their system into his United Fighting

Arts curriculum. The Machados now supervise the program under which second- and third-degree black belts acquire practical grappling skills.

Another major difference exists between what the brothers teach and what other Brazilian instructors teach in Brazil and the United States. "Since coming here, we have developed a different approach," John says. "We try to work on different techniques and meet different people—like [judo instructor] Gene LeBell and [small-circle jujutsu instructor] Wally Jay—to bring good things to jiu-jitsu, such as incorporating new techniques from professional wrestling, freestyle wrestling, sambo and judo."

"We don't believe martial arts are a package; you have to keep changing," John continues. "We keep working to make our system grow and evolve. We don't have a package—a book that we follow for 10 years. Every six months, we change to see what works best in the learning process."

"We don't change the principles of the art; we change by improving it and bringing new things in," Carlos says. "The techniques are adaptable, and it has to be that way. I have no doubt that 10 years ago techniques were a little bit different from what they are today, and that 10 years from now they will be slightly different from what they are today."

The Machados say student enrollment has grown steadily during the past few years because jiu-jitsu is gaining fame in the United States. They say students want to try the Brazilian grappling art after reading magazine articles about it. "Also, our students bring in a lot of others, a lot of friends," Carlos says. "Once students get acquainted with what we do and get comfortable with it, they want to show somebody else."

Besides these five brothers, no one else in the United States teaches the Machado brand of jiu-jitsu. "But we have some assistants we are preparing—Renato Magno and Bob Bass," John says. The Machados currently operate two schools in California—one in Redondo Beach and one in Encino—but they plan to expand soon. "Eventually, we will open schools in the San Diego area and Santa Barbara," John adds.

The Machados have had offers of sponsorship to open schools in many areas, including Texas, Australia, Japan, Holland and Brazil, but so far, they have declined. They prefer to remain together near a place—in this case, Los Angeles—where they can accomplish their goals, which include spreading their philosophical martial art and breaking into movies and television.

"We worked in *Kickboxer 4*, which will come out on video soon," John says. "We used a lot of jiu-jitsu in it, and we helped in the choreography." John will also have a role in the upcoming feature film *Heatseeker*, and Carlos helped choreograph Norris' fight scenes in an episode of *Walker, Texas Ranger*. He even appeared briefly in the episode. "If you follow that series, you can notice that a lot of chokes, armbars and things familiar to jiu-jitsu are being shown," Carlos says.

Because of the publicity, the Machado brothers predict an expansion of Brazilian jiu-jitsu in the United States. "We are one of the pioneers in the teaching of Brazilian jiu-jitsu," John says. "We are opening doors for other people to eventually come [from Brazil]."

John Machado

Brazil on the East Coast

Logically, the generic term "Brazilian jiu-jitsu" should apply to any form of jiu-jitsu from Brazil. In the United States, however, at least one person, New Jersey-based Craig Kukuk, has had to adopt the term to describe the grappling art he teaches and thus avoid the legal problems that would have resulted from using the Gracie name.

The Summer/Fall 1992 issue of the *Gracie Jiu-Jitsu Newsletter* says: "Our student and friend Craig Kukuk has become the first American to receive a black belt in Gracie jiu-jitsu. He is going through an instructor's program at the Gracie Academy in Torrance, California. Upon completion of this program, he will be teaching on the East Coast."

But because Rorion now distinguishes the grappling art and the unique way it is taught, he said Kukuk did not receive a black belt in Gracie jiu-jitsu. "He was awarded a black belt in jiu-jitsu by Rorion Gracie," he says instead. "Craig entered the program with us but is no longer following the same instruction that I gave him. Craig is not teaching Gracie jiu-jitsu; he's teaching jiu-jitsu his way."

Kukuk says he received a black belt from Royler and his father, Helio, in Brazil while being groomed as an instructor. "I returned to the United States and went through an instructor's program, taught for six months in the Los Angeles [Gracie] Academy and received a diploma," he says. But because of his relationship with the Gracie Jiu-Jitsu Academy, Kukuk says he does not honor that rank. He is currently certified by the Renzo Gracie Academy of Brazil, he says.

Kukuk has trained in Brazilian jiu-jitsu for 11 years, both in the United States and Brazil. Since relocating to the Professional Karate Academy in Red Bank, New Jersey, and organizing new classes, Kukuk has not altered any significant aspects or techniques of the popular art. "I just try to keep it like I learned it—for the street fight and not for sport," he says.

Like other Brazilian jiu-jitsu instructors in America, Kukuk admits to a growing public interest after last year's Ultimate Fighting Championship. "We saw a definite increase in our student base," he says. Unfortunately for East Coast martial arts students, Kukuk has no immediate plans to expand. "I teach six days a week in Princeton, New Jersey; Red Bank, New Jersey; and New York City," he says. "So I am not planning on teaching any more than that for a while."

"I look forward to [training my own instructors]," Kukuk says. "But you must remember that Brazilian jiu-jitsu has been in the United States for 20 years, and I'm the only American to become a black belt and a teacher. So I'm not holding my breath for the next one."

Monteiro Jiu-jitsu

Still another independent instructor, Nelson Monteiro, teaches the grappling art in Del Mar, California, just north of San Diego. A native of Rio de Janeiro, Brazil, Monteiro studied under Carlos Gracie Jr. for more than 10 years and now displays numerous medals and trophies from Brazilian tournaments. In 1985, Monteiro graduated from Rio's Gama Filho University with a degree in physical education, and in 1989 he moved to Southern California.

Monteiro says phone calls from prospective students have increased because of the publicity Brazilian jiu-jitsu now receives. He estimates 20 percent of those callers mention the jiu-jitsu victory at the Ultimate Fighting Championship.

Like the others who studied under the Gracie patriarchs, Monteiro offers instruction in Brazilian jiu-jitsu and nutrition counseling. He teaches jiu-jitsu to members of the Carlsbad Police Department in California and hopes to expand into San Diego.

The pioneering work of the Gracie family has opened up possibilities for thousands of American martial artists to learn Brazilian jiu-jitsu. Whether you study under a Gracie, a Machado, a Kukuk or a Monteiro, you can rest assured this realistic ground-fighting art from South America will greatly enhance your self-defense capabilities.

ROYCE GRACIE WINS UFC—AGAIN
by Douglas Jeffrey • Karate/Kung Fu Illustrated • August 1994

Can anyone beat Royce Gracie? Thus far, there have been two Ultimate Fighting Championships, and Gracie has won both. In the first UFC, he defeated three opponents. In the second UFC, the promoters doubled the field to 16 fighters, which meant the winner would have to fight four times rather than three. Nevertheless, Gracie disposed of his opponents in record time. In fact, during the two events, he has probably fought a total of 10 minutes—and earned $110,000.

When the 27-year-old Rio de Janeiro, Brazil, native entered the octagonal ring at the Mammoth Event Center in Denver, on March 11, 1994, he was all business. In his first match, the 6-foot-1-inch, 176-pound Gracie squared off against Minoki Ichihara, a *daido-juku* karate stylist from Tokyo. Gracie threw a couple of front kicks toward Ichihara's knee, then bolted in and took down his 25-year-old opponent. Gracie immediately mounted the 5-foot-6-1/2-inch, 176-pound Ichihara and threw several head and body punches.

After a brief struggle in which Ichihara almost escaped, Gracie mounted him again, threw some more punches and applied a choke. Soon afterward, Ichihara, who had a full-contact record of 56-4 with 20 knockouts, tapped out.

In his next bout, Gracie faced Jason DeLucia, who was determined to beat the *jiu-jitsu* stylist, especially after he lost to him two years ago in a nontournament match at the Gracie Jiu-Jitsu Academy in Torrance, California. "It is nothing personal," DeLucia said before the fight. "He is a gentleman, respectable and admirable, as is the whole family. I just want to beat Royce. When he beat me [before], I was ignorant. And yes, he can be beaten. [Royce's brother] Rickson is more dominant."

DeLucia, a five-animal kung fu stylist from Bellingham, Massachusetts, advanced to the quarterfinals against Gracie by defeating Scott Baker, a *wing chun* kung fu stylist from Provo, Utah. DeLucia's bout with Gracie was another story, however.

DeLucia opened with a front kick that missed, and Gracie immediately took him down and mounted him. The fighters struggled to the fence surrounding the octagon. DeLucia turned Gracie over and stood up, while Gracie wrapped his legs around DeLucia's neck. In the skirmish, Gracie managed to apply an armbar on his 24-year-old opponent, forcing him to tap out.

After the fight, DeLucia said the fence helped Gracie. "I executed a bridge and roll, but the fence kept him from rolling," said DeLucia, who has also trained in judo for more than 10 years. "I am not disappointed he won. I am disappointed with the environment. Without the fence, the fight would not have ended. Up until that point, I was in control. Next time, I am going to drag him to the center of the ring, so when I roll him on his back, he won't have anything to stop him. He will be in trouble if that happens again."

Gracie saw things differently, however. "If he comes back, I'll beat him again," Gracie said. "In fact, he can come over anytime. He doesn't have to wait for the tournament. I'll do the same move or another one. I will tighten the screws every time. I love guys who make excuses."

DeLucia—who plans to train with shootfighter Ken Shamrock, another fighter who vows to beat Gracie the next time they meet—said he is familiar with Gracie's maneuvers. "I know his system and the ways to beat him," DeLucia said.

Gracie, however, said his experience will make it tough for DeLucia. "While one country is building a rocket ship to go to the moon, where do you think the Americans are planning to send their next rocket ship?" Gracie asked. "By the time [DeLucia] gets [to the moon], I will be way over there. I will have different ways to beat him."

After defeating DeLucia, Gracie advanced to the semifinals against Remco Pardoel, the 1993 International Ju-Jitsu Federation world heavyweight Danish, Belgium, German and Dutch open champion.

Pardoel, who is 6 feet 3-3/4 inches tall and weighs 260 pounds, defeated Alberto Cerro Leon, a *pentjak silat* stylist from Lemoa, Spain, and Orlando Weit, a Thai boxer from France, to advance.

In his match with Weit, Pardoel took his smaller opponent down and lay on his back across Weit's chest. Weit struggled but could not budge Pardoel. Finally, Pardoel blasted Weit, the 1991 and 1993 world Thai boxing champion, with seven elbow strikes to the head, and Weit's corner threw in the towel.

After the fight, Pardoel said his strategy was to take down Weit as quickly as possible. "He can kick and punch with the best of them," said the 24-year-old Dutchman. "When I saw that opening, I knew that was my chance. I am a big guy, and throwing elbows at that distance works fine."

Things did not work so well for Pardoel against Gracie, who eliminated him in about one minute. Gracie faked a couple of front kicks, then charged in and grabbed him around the midsection. Pardoel resisted at first, but Gracie wrestled him to the ground and choked him with the collar of his uniform.

Despite his size advantage, Pardoel said he could not escape. "I wasn't tired, but he had a choke on my artery, which prevents blood from getting to my brain," said Pardoel, who earned $5,000 from the event. "It was a hopeless position for me. Next time, I hope to give him a better fight."

Gracie's victory set up the final against Patrick Smith of Aurora, Colorado, who quickly overcame his previous opponents. In his first match, Smith—a kickboxer with black belts in *tang soo do, taekwondo, enshin* karate and *hapkido*—disposed of Ray Wizard, a *kenpo* stylist from Los Angeles.

In his second, Smith squared off against Scott Morris, an American *ninjutsu* stylist from North Richland Hills, Texas. Morris, a part-time instructor with Robert Bussey's Warrior International, charged at Smith, who grabbed the 6-foot, 208-pound Morris and took him to the ground. Smith, 30, immediately began pounding Morris with elbow smashes and punches to the head, which bloodied Morris' face. He required 24 stitches afterward.

After the fight, Smith, who has a professional kickboxing record of 10-0 with eight knockouts, told reporter Herb Perez that he was going to roll over his next opponent. "I'll be right on top of him, and I will pound him," Smith said moments after his victory.

Smith did not pound Johnny Rhodes, his next opponent, but he did dispose of the *shorinji-ryu* karate stylist from Las Vegas fairly quickly. At 39, Rhodes was the oldest competitor, but this did not prevent him from defeating his first two opponents convincingly.

In his first match, Rhodes, who also earned $5,000, defeated wing chun stylist David Levicki. The fight was unique for two reasons: As the longest match, it lasted 16 minutes, and Rhodes kept losing his pants.

After Rhodes mounted the 6-foot-5-inch, 275-pound Levicki, the fighters exchanged punches. In an attempt to escape, Levicki, a resident of Orem, Utah, tried to remove Rhodes by wrapping his legs around his waist and pushing. Each time he did, however, Rhodes' pants came down, exposing his buttocks. And each time that happened, the referee pulled Rhodes' pants back up.

Levicki said he was trying to push Rhodes with his feet. "Each time I put my feet on his hips, he slid down," Levicki said. "Each time I did this, though, his pants slid off, too. When the referee pulled his pants back up, he pulled Rhodes back on top of me." Finally, Levicki, 28, tapped out because Rhodes' punches had caused his face to bleed profusely.

Rhodes was completely serious in his semifinal bout with Smith, and he had to be, considering the way Smith had steamrolled his previous opponents. The fighters exchanged some harmless kicks and punches, then Smith bolted in, pinned Rhodes against the fence, applied a standing choke and won.

Smith's victory set up the final against Gracie. As Smith entered the ring, the crowd went crazy for the hometown kickboxer. Seconds later, Gracie entered the octagon, and the crowd booed. When the crowd finished booing Gracie, they chanted, "Patrick, Patrick, Patrick." When Gracie was formally introduced, they booed again.

When the match started, the fighters circled, each waiting for the other to initiate. The second Smith tried a front kick, Gracie charged in, took him down and threw three rights to Smith's face. Seconds later, Smith's corner threw in the towel.

Rickson Gracie, Royce's cornerman, said he was not surprised by the quick towel. "Actually, they were smart," Rickson said. "If they hadn't [thrown it in, Smith] would have received more damage, and he would have just wasted his energy by fighting."

Royce, who sustained a small scratch under his right eye in the finals, said his strategy was to let Smith, who earned $15,000, make the first move. "Rickson said to let Smith come to me," Royce said. "As soon as he kicked or punched, I was going to take him down," said Royce, adding that the crowd's booing did not bother him. "Rickson told me not to worry about it. He said it is good to fight against the crowd."

Royce said he did not watch Smith's fights on closed-circuit television, but his brothers made him aware that he would be facing the 6-foot-2-inch, 219-pound Smith in the finals. "They said he improved a lot," Royce said. "But besides my brothers, no one has given me any trouble yet. Smith learned some grappling, but he knows he can [not] grapple with me. Once I closed the distance on him and took him down, I could tell by the look on his face that the fight was over."

Gracie's victory proved satisfying for his entire family, including his father, Helio Gracie, who watched from a ringside seat. Through an interpreter, Helio said he was proud of Royce. "I feel great, and I am not surprised," he said. "I don't feel like anyone else is at our [skill] level. I am confident that only an accident or a surprise hit would have beaten Royce."

Co-promoter Arthur Davie was also pleased—for a different reason. More than 99,000 households subscribed to the first pay-per-view UFC in November 1993, and there was a 10 percent to 15 percent increase this time, he said.

The matches have certainly generated excitement throughout the martial arts world, but some have questioned the quality of the fighters.

Co-promoter Rorion Gracie said the UFC gives everyone an opportunity to back up his claims. "We have been in the martial arts for a long time, and I know it is impossible to make everybody agree with you all the time," he said. "Even if Royce wins 10 out of 10, they will say, 'What if Bruce Lee was alive?' My feeling is, the octagon is a way for people to put up or shut up. It is as simple as that. This is the perfect venue for people to show what they claim to be able to do. This is an honest, straightforward way to handle it."

For the second time, Royce certainly seemed to handle it without any problems. Asked after the event whether it was more difficult facing an extra fighter this time, Royce replied, "I can feel my muscles. I am tired, but I feel like a champion."

And no one can dispute that—at least for now.

HELIO GRACIE, THE FATHER OF BRAZILIAN JIU-JITSU
Karate/Kung Fu Illustrated • August 1994

The Gracies claim that their devastating style of *jiu-jitsu* derives its unbeatable techniques from modifications made by Helio Gracie. In this exclusive interview, the 81-year-old patriarch of the Gracie clan—who still teaches two or three classes a day—discusses his life, his art and the Ultimate Fighting Championship.

Karate/Kung Fu Illustrated: Could you explain the roles you and your brother, Carlos Gracie, had in the creation of Gracie jiu-jitsu?

Helio Gracie: Carlos was a student of Count Koma, who brought Japanese *jujutsu* [to Brazil]. Because I was weak and small, Carlos didn't teach me. So I would watch Carlos' classes, and I learned jujutsu from watching. That was in 1929 and 1930.

KKI: When did you begin watching Carlos Gracie's classes, and when did you take over his classes?

Helio: When I started watching his classes, I was about 13 or 14. One year and a half later, I started teaching.

KKI: When in your jujutsu training did you decide the art's techniques needed modification?

Helio: I didn't invent the martial art. I adapted it to my necessity—what I needed for my weight and lack of strength. I learned jujutsu, but some of the moves required a lot of strength, so I could not use them. I couldn't get out from some of the positions I learned from my brother because of my lack of strength and weight. So I developed other ways out.

KKI: Why didn't anyone before you refine the techniques of traditional jujutsu into a more effective style?

Helio: Because most people who practice martial arts already have the physical strength and ability that I didn't have. I needed to create those [techniques]. This is the only way I had to compensate for my lack of strength.

KKI: Could you tell us your age, height and weight?

Helio: I am 81 and [almost 5 feet 9 inches] tall. I have never weighed more than [139 pounds]; right now I am [132 pounds].

KKI: Do any members of your family still compete in Brazilian tournaments to prove the style's effectiveness?

Helio: There are competitions at the sport level, but we don't need [to fight] anymore to prove our point in Brazil because there's no doubt about the effectiveness of Gracie jiu-jitsu. The tournaments [the family participates in] are sport competitions in jiu-jitsu. There are [real, no-holds-barred] fights in Brazil, but the Gracies don't need to prove anything else there because we already proved the point by going 65 years undefeated.

KKI: No one challenges you anymore?
Helio: No one has the courage to do that.

KKI: Besides the Gracie Challenge, what is the difference between Gracie jiu-jitsu and the other styles of jiu-jitsu in Brazil?
Helio: First, there are no other styles of jiu-jitsu in Brazil. The only branch in Brazil is the one that came from me. There are different scales and different levels—people who learned more and teach more efficiently, and bad instructors who didn't learn from me. There are good teachers and bad teachers, but they all come from Gracie jiu-jitsu. The difference between [Brazilian jiu-jitsu here and in Brazil] is that in the United States, [we're] the only ones teaching Gracie jiu-jitsu. So that's why we are on top—the other ones are different. Almost everyone knows Gracie jiu-jitsu in Brazil; the difference is, who knows more. Since it came from the Gracie family and me, the people closest to me know more. The people who are farther away and from lower branches [of the family] know less.

KKI: Why did you start the Gracie Challenge?
Helio: Because I really believed in Gracie jiu-jitsu. How could I prove this art was the best art? If I say I can speak English, I need to prove it by entering into conversation. It's the same with the art. I believed Gracie jiu-jitsu was the best, and if someone doubted that, I was willing to [prove it].

KKI: How do you respond to people who criticize martial arts challenges as being contrary to the spirit of the martial arts?
Helio: When people don't want to [match] what they know [against what others know], it is generally because they don't believe in what they are doing. [If you wanted to show the public] what the best martial art is, what would you say? How would you prove your point? How would you compare one to the other [without style-versus-style matches]? I believe there's a need for the martial arts to confront each other so the public can observe them and see which is more effective. About the spirit of martial arts—we don't need to hit; we don't need to punch; we don't need to hurt our opponent. Although we can, we don't need to. The only way to show people is [through these matches]. That's why we're doing the Ultimate Fighting Championship—to show people we can subdue our opponents

41

without kicking, without punching, without hurting. It's hard to draw a conclusion [about which art is best unless] you have an event in which you put karate against *taekwondo* and [other styles]. But in the United States, you don't have that type of competition. We wanted to bring this here because millions of people practice martial arts, and sometimes they get hurt. But this is not necessary to know how to fight.

KKI: But what about people who say the challenges go against the spirit of the martial arts?

Helio: If you get someone who [does not know about the no-holds-barred event] and put him in the ring and beat him up, that's against the spirit. But we're dealing with professional fighters. And the only way you can compare martial arts with different rules—without favoring one style—is to [use] a no-rules system. I don't believe the belief [you just mentioned] about the Gracie Challenge is common in the martial arts community. A lot of good, respected martial arts instructors are learning with the Gracie family. And how would you have known of the effectiveness of Gracie jiu-jitsu if you didn't [see one style matched against another] in the championship? Everything in life has to be proved. The only way to prove a martial art works is in a fight.

KKI: Is it true that a Gracie jiu-jitsu practitioner does not need speed or strength to beat an opponent?

Helio: If the opponent knows Gracie jiu-jitsu, then the physical characteristics could make a difference. If he doesn't know Gracie jiu-jitsu, then it's true. Gracie jiu-jitsu will lose only to Gracie jiu-jitsu. The reason is that jiu-jitsu is richer; it has more resources. All martial arts are good and effective, but some produce more than others. As far as I know, jiu-jitsu is the only one [for which this is true]. Jiu-jitsu is strong where other martial arts are weak. We don't apply a hold or technique; we ask for it—give it the conditions to work.

KKI: What future do you see for Gracie jiu-jitsu?

Helio: When I see the support from the martial arts community in the United States and the way it's growing, I see it as a great thing—a great future for us, the Americans who learn it and the rest of the world. I wish I had 100 sons so I could [spread the art] faster.

STILL KING OF THE HILL

by Sandra E. Kessler • Photo by Rick Hustead • Black Belt • August 1994

When Royce Gracie won the first "no-holds-barred" Ultimate Fighting Championship, he turned a few heads but couldn't erase centuries-old beliefs that held that the best fighters in the martial arts were those who kicked and punched, not those who choked and wrestled around on the ground.

When the 27-year-old Brazilian *jiu-jitsu* stylist defended his title, beating four fighters from essentially striking self-defense systems, even staunch martial arts traditionalists couldn't help but take notice. How, they wondered, could a 180-pound grappler so easily dispense with such hard-hitting fighters who outweighed him by nearly 100 pounds?

The answer, Royce says, is simple: Gracie jiu-jitsu is the most effective fighting art in the world today. And he points to his two titles and 7-0 record in UFC competition as evidence of that. He has fought for about 10 minutes combined in the two tournaments and has yet to break a sweat, earning a reported $110,000 for his "efforts." Can anybody beat this guy?

Sure, Royce says. His brother, Rickson Gracie, can. But Royce doubts anyone outside the Gracie jiu-jitsu family has a chance in Hades of dislodging him from the top of the martial arts mountain. And he tells you why in the following interview, as he reflects on his UFC victories, reveals his fighting strategy, and explains why he deserves more respect from his peers.

Black Belt: The biggest criticism of the first two Ultimate Fighting Championships has centered on the quality of your opponents. Most of the fighters haven't exactly been household names and, at the last tournament, two were fast approaching 40 years of age. Therefore, some people don't think you have proved anything with your two victories, and they are wondering when you are going to face some real competition.

Royce Gracie: The invitation [to compete at the event] is [open] to everybody. It's not my fault that someone doesn't want to come here if they're scared. But the invitation's for all the Mike Tysons, Chuck Norrises and Evander Holyfields [in the world]. The guys who got into the tournament are supposed to be good in their styles. They are all tough guys. It doesn't matter who I beat, they're always going to say, "Well, that's not a really tough guy." When I beat [UFC runner-up] Pat Smith, they probably said, "Oh, Pat Smith is easy." But he trashed all his opponents in 30 seconds. They don't give credit to me.

BB: Do the UFC promoters, one of whom is your older brother Rorion, actively recruit big-name martial artists?

Royce: We have recruited people. We talked to [kickboxing champion] Dennis Alexio. We placed a call to [kickboxing champion] Benny Urquidez. We talked to [kickboxing champion] Stan Longinidis. We talked to [former kickboxing champion] Jean-Yves Theriault. Those are some of the top names in the martial arts. And for whatever reason, they couldn't do it or

Royce Gracie

didn't want to do it. So what else can we do? I can't go to their house and pull them out of their beds and throw them on the mat.

BB: Do you think it's fair that your brother Rorion ultimately decides who gets to fight in the UFC?

Royce: Somebody has to choose who fights. He's always trying to look for the best fighters in the world. We're waiting for the big names. I guess we have to call somebody from Mars next time. Where are the tough guys? We can't wait to get applications from them.

BB: Of your seven UFC bouts, which has been the most difficult?

Royce: The opponent who gave me the hardest time was myself, my mind. What I'm more concerned about is the guys who keep talking about how they can beat me. I don't see them [at the tournament]; I only see them in [martial arts] magazines. They say they can beat me, and that it's easy to stop me. Where are they? They keep saying they can beat me, but they don't show up [at the tournament]. There is no excuse for any tough guy in the world not to show up. Martial arts students who hear from their instructors how deadly their style is should say, "Hey, teacher, how come you don't step into the octagon at the Ultimate Fighting Championship? Go in there and show how good you are."

BB: So you don't have any objection to fighting the world's best kick-boxers?

Royce: Tell them to show up. Ultimately, the martial arts are about self-defense, about effectiveness. People keep claiming to be effective, but they're not willing to step up and prove it.

BB: You have certainly earned respect in one corner of the world. Since you beat their fighter, Minoki Ichihara, at the second UFC, the Japanese media has given you extensive coverage.

Royce: They say that I'm the No. 1 man in Japan. If I go over there, the red carpet will roll. They are giving me much more credit than everybody else. They can't believe that as slight as I am, I can beat guys who are 220, 230 or 260 pounds. They give me total credit. The day I lose, they might take it away. But until then, I'm the king.

BB: What is your fighting strategy? Do you always wait for your opponent to make the first move, then charge in before he can set up for another technique?

Royce: Sometimes I just come in, and sometimes I wait. It's just timing. There is no secret to it. I just get in a clinch. I'm not in a hurry. Sometimes I just want to get it over with, and sometimes I want to take my time.

BB: Were your opponents better prepared for your grappling tactics at the second UFC?

Royce: I noticed they were prepared. They were very scared of the choke from behind. But they forget that I can go for arm locks, foot locks, knees, wrists and different types of chokes. They tried to protect against one choke but forgot about the rest.

BB: Has anyone connected with a solid blow in your seven UFC fights?

Royce: Not yet. I duck really quickly.

BB: Patrick Smith, the fighter you beat for the second UFC title, tapped out before you got a good lock on him or were able to hit him much. Why do you think he gave up so quickly?

Royce: He's a smart guy. He's not a grappler, so once he's on the ground, he's smart to quit so fast. If he knows he has no chance at it, why keep fighting? If I'm going to play basketball against Michael Jordan, I have no chance. Why should I play? [Smith] knew he didn't have a chance. There's no reason to get his face split apart.

BB: Do you think a Brazilian jiu-jitsu stylist like yourself would have a good chance of beating you?

Royce: There's only one way to find out.

BB: Why, when you have so many talented brothers, were you chosen as the Gracie family's representative for these fights?

Royce: [My brother] Rickson is the champion of the family. He's the one who can beat everybody. The matches would not be fair if Rickson fought. He is 10 times better than me. If I can do what I'm doing [at the tournaments], imagine if Rickson was there. So they decided to give me a chance to do it.

BB: Your tournament victories have been great publicity for Gracie jiu-jitsu and have helped legitimize the family's claims that its art is the most effective fighting system in the world. If you should lose one day, will that likewise hurt the style's credibility?

Royce: I'm human; I'm not bulletproof. If I get hit—a good hit—it can knock me out. I'm putting my money where my mouth is. Everybody else claims to have deadly styles, but they don't have the guts to come [to the tournament] and prove it. At least I'm willing to step up and show my students that what I'm teaching, I'm willing to prove and willing to believe in. I'm taking a chance. I'm putting my neck on the guillotine. Nobody else backs up their claims. Some people who teach [a similar style of] Brazilian jiu-jitsu called me after the first UFC, and again after the second UFC, and said, "Retire, Royce. Because if you lose, we lose. You're the champion, you're the man, so why fight again? Just quit." They're afraid that if I lose, the style might lose.

BB: How important is it to you to uphold the 65-year Gracie family tradition of dominance in no-holds-barred challenge fights?
Royce: It's my life. I would die for that.

BB: That's a lot of pressure. Do you ever worry about losing?
Royce: No. I know what I can do. I know what I did already. Who else in the world fought four guys in one night, four champions, and beat them all? The Gracie name has come a long way. It was built on the sweat and blood of my father, Helio. It wasn't because we are nice guys. If I was worried about losing, I wouldn't enter the ring; I'd stay home. I'd retire.

BB: Does it bother you that some people just don't want to admit that their self-defense system is vulnerable to grappling and ground-fighting tactics?
Royce: It's just not politically correct to come out and say some martial arts aren't as efficient as they claim to be. Everybody started to get upset because now we are hurting them in their pocketbooks. More than ever, people are realizing that other martial arts are not as effective as they claim to be. They give people a false sense of security. You must know how to fight on the ground, or you're in deep yogurt during a fight.

BB: Because you and your brothers believe so deeply in the effectiveness of your fighting system, some people think that you come off as cocky and arrogant. Are you worried about the family image?
Royce: I'm not concerned about it. People can think whatever they want to think. I know who I am. The confidence that we have about jiu-jitsu being the best is what hurts some people. It's not that we're trying to brag; we are just extremely confident. Our intention in talking strongly about jiu-jitsu with the conviction that we do is not to put anybody else down; it's because we want to be sure that we are heard. If we don't make any noise, we'll just be another martial art lost in the crowd. So we make noise, but we are willing to back up the noise. That should not be looked at as a wrong kind of attitude. It should be seen as extreme confidence in what we do.

BB: Are you saying you can't be beaten?
Royce: Everybody loses one day.

BB: How similar is the UFC to the open challenge matches in which the Gracie family members were involved in Brazil?

Royce: Back in Brazil, it was more personal. And we didn't have managers setting up the fights. The two fighters set it up right there: "I don't like you, you don't like me. Let's fight." Now we are making it an event; we are recruiting fighters from all around the world.

BB: Before you won your UFC titles, few people knew your name. Now, all of a sudden, you—excuse the pun—"grace" the pages of just about every martial arts magazine. Has your sudden fame changed you?

Royce: No, not at all. You know what I was doing right before you came here? I was cleaning the bathroom. So I guess I haven't changed much.

BB: There has been speculation that, because you won the two UFC titles, your brother Rorion, who co-promoted both events, didn't have to award the championship purses of $50,000 and $60,000. Have you received, and cashed, both checks?

Royce: Yes, I am getting [the money]. If you want to find out whether you get paid, enter the tournament.

BB: The two paydays are among the highest ever awarded for a martial arts championship.

Royce: Let's make sure it stays that way. Let's keep going a little higher.

BB: Some traditional *jujutsu* stylists have suggested you are misrepresenting the so-called "gentle art" because of your aggressive fighting style.

Royce: Wait. Did I break anybody's face? Did I hurt anybody that bad? I've been gentle with [my opponents]. I punch very softly, just to wear them out. I'm not trying to break their faces. I'm being as gentle as I can be. It's almost like fighting my sister. In fact, my sister doesn't cry as much as they do. They complain so much.

BB: Is your style of jiu-jitsu different from traditional jujutsu?

Royce: Yes, it is. That's why we call it Gracie jiu-jitsu. What happens is that we have the same arm locks, chokes and foot locks that any good judo man or any traditional jujutsu man has. The difference is the transition from one position to another position—we have become extremely proficient at that. Fluidity is important. It's like rice—you cook yours for 10 minutes, I cook mine for 15 minutes, but it's still rice. We just put a little more pepper, a little more salt in ours. Our rice is very spicy. It's a matter of taste. It's not that it's a different art, we just present it a little differently.

BB: Any chance that you will step down in the near future and let one of your brothers represent Gracie jiu-jitsu at the Ultimate Fighting Championship?

Royce: It could happen that one of my brothers would replace me. I guess since I fought in the first one, the pay-per-view cable people want to keep me until I lose. When I lose, they'll bring in another brother.

ROYCE GRACIE'S CONDITIONING PROGRAM

by Douglas Jeffrey • *Martial Arts Training* • November 1994

The Ultimate Fighting Championship has the martial arts world buzzing. Some say Royce Gracie's challengers are too old. Others say his opponents are mediocre fighters. Some say the rules favor grappling.

You can argue these points forever, but there are two points that are irrefutable. First, Gracie is the Ultimate Fighting Champion. Second, the 27-year-old *jiu-jitsu* stylist is in shape.

If you're skeptical of either point, consider this. First, Gracie won both Ultimate Fighting Championships. Second, Gracie defeated all his opponents in Denver, the Mile High City. And the elevation apparently did not bother him too much. After the second UFC, Gracie said he "could feel his muscles," but he would fight another opponent if he had to.

Is this man in shape or what?

How does he do it?

Besides having an incredible amount of talent, the Rio de Janeiro, Brazil, native lifts weights, stretches constantly, follows a special nutritional program, and does a brutal cardiovascular workout that will tire some people out just thinking about it.

Before we take you through Gracie's training routine, tighten your seat belt, take a deep breath and hold on. This is definitely not for the fainthearted.

Cardiovascular Routine

To stay in shape, Gracie uses a rowing machine, rides a stationary bicycle, jumps rope, swims and runs on the beach. His Monday workout begins with 30 minutes of stationary bicycling.

"I maintain a fast pace," Gracie says. "I can't cruise on a bike."

When he's done, he jumps on the rowing machine for 15 minutes. Again, the pace is fast. When finished, he heads to the beach. And, you guessed it, the pace is fast. His two-mile run on the soft sand usually takes about 18 minutes. Why is the pace always fast?

"I like the fast pace," Gracie says. "I never thought much about it; I just do it. I don't have much time, so I have to get done quickly."

Gracie repeats this routine Wednesdays and Fridays.

Tuesdays and Thursdays, he swims—to relax.

"Weightlifting makes my muscles tight," Gracie says. "Therefore, I swim on the days I lift to loosen my muscles and relax."

The pace? What else.

"I swim for about half an hour, and I swim fast, even though it might be slow to someone else," he says, laughing.

His cardiovascular routine does not end on Fridays. He also jumps rope for 10 minutes on Saturdays and Sundays.

"The pace is fast, always fast," he says.

Gracie also hits speed bags and heavy bags on weekends.

"I do this just to play around," Gracie says. "Both of these are good for coordination."

Eric Mickley, Gracie's fitness trainer, says the UFC champion's program is impressive.

"He's like the Energizer Bunny," Mickley says. "He keeps going and going and going."

Gracie's cardiovascular fitness is important because one of the UFC bouts may keep going and going, says Mickley, pointing out that Gracie's father, Helio Gracie, once fought for three hours and 45 minutes.

"What if Royce ends up in a nightmare like that?" Mickley says. "He needs the aerobics."

If a fight does last awhile, Gracie says he is ready.

"I fought four guys in the second Ultimate Fighting Championship, and that is a lot," Gracie says. "It is a lot. But if you put five guys out there, I will fight. I know they are getting tired, too. [At that point,] we are on the same level. And my technique is better, so I will beat them."

Weight Training

Gracie, who pumps iron twice per week, began lifting weights before the second UFC because he is always looking for ways to improve.

"More than twice a week would be overtraining," Mickley says. "It's better to undertrain than overtrain."

Furthermore, if weight training is going to be effective, the muscles have to recover, says Mickley, the 1991 California powerlifting champion.

"If you train six days a week, you are tearing your muscles down without giving them a chance to recover," he says. "When you lift, you are stressing your muscle fibers, your nervous system and many other things. You have to let your body recuperate so it heals stronger."

Gracie's routine—which builds speed, power and endurance—is geared specifically for jiu-jitsu.

"We are working the muscles that he uses in jiu-jitsu," Mickley says. "We are not making him a powerlifter. We are making him a better jiu-jitsu fighter."

And they are doing that with compensatory acceleration training, a system in which Gracie lifts 80 percent of his maximum weight as fast as possible.

"To develop speed and strength, Royce uses heavy weights with less repetitions, and he pushes the weights up as fast as he can," Mickley says. "Then, he lowers the weights at a normal speed. Lifting heavy weights with explosive movements works the fast-twitch muscle fibers. Therefore, when Royce lifts, he usually does four sets of five repetitions. If he can do more than five repetitions, he doesn't have enough weight on the bar for power training."

Studies show compensatory acceleration training makes people stronger, Mickley says.

"Some of the world's best powerlifters are using this," he says. "It really develops speed and power, which are vital in athletics."

It should not be surprising that Gracie prefers a fast-paced workout.

"It was a struggle when I first started training with him because he wanted to do a set every 15 seconds," Mickley says. "I had to drum it into him that the longer he waits, the more weight he can handle. And the more weight he can handle, the stronger and faster he is going to get."

Gracie lifts weights Tuesdays and Thursdays, and he begins by warming up.

"The best way to warm up is to do the exercise you are going to do real slow," says Mickley. "For example, the best way to warm up for the squat is to do a squat. Royce just uses the bar. This prepares his body for the exercise, and it's unlikely he'll get hurt."

Gracie's workout usually lasts only 60 to 90 minutes because he does super-sets. He does two exercises consecutively, rests for five minutes and repeats the routine.

"When he takes a break, he is fresh and strong for the next lift," Mickley says. "He can really explode when he does the next lift. This really works power. If we were working endurance, I'd have him go, go, go. There would not be any breaks."

On Tuesdays, Gracie usually focuses on the upper body. He performs the bench press, French press and T-bar row, which are known as pushing exercises. He also does some endurance exercises such as biceps curls, which are known as pulling exercises.

To begin, Gracie does a super-set of bench presses and curls. Next, he does a super-set of T-bar rows for endurance, then french presses, which strengthen the triceps.

On Thursdays, he normally works the lower body. Occasionally, however, he repeats exercises from the previous workout with less weight.

"When you do light exercises after a heavy workout, your muscles heal better than if you do nothing," Mickley says. "If you bench heavy one day a week and real light the other day, you are going to gain mass quicker because you are increasing the blood flow to the muscle, which helps it heal faster."

When Gracie works his lower body, he does squats, dead lifts and calf raises. If he feels pain while working out, Gracie skips the exercise for that body part.

"The long-term benefits are more important than the short-term benefits," Mickley says. "If he lifts with mediocre intensity for five years, he'll be better off than if he lifts really hard for six months and gets injured or quits because he doesn't like it. I want him to like weightlifting and lift the rest of his life."

To ensure safety, Mickley strictly enforces technique.

Gracie maintains a comfortable stance, keeps his weight on his heels, his knees lined up over his feet, his butt down, and his back arched.

"I don't want him to put too much strain on his knees," Mickley says. "I want him to distribute the pressure evenly between his knees, hips and lower back."

It's also important to squat low, Mickley says.

"Depth is important," Mickley says. "His butt has to drop below his knees. If he does not do it right, I make him do one more. I want him to get good."

When Gracie does curls, he keeps his back, head and butt against a wall.

"I don't want him to lean when he is lifting because he can strain his back," Mickley says. "Besides, if he leans, that is cheating, ineffective and potentially dangerous."

Gracie always uses barbells rather than dumbbells because he can lift more weight, Mickley says.

"You can't overload dumbbells," he says. "When you can go heavier, you'll get stronger."

While lifting, Gracie keeps his butt, shoulders and head on the bench, and his feet on the ground. He uses a wide grip, lowers the bar to his chest ,and arches his back slightly so he can lift more weight.

"If he holds the bar too narrow, it works the triceps," Mickley says.

To prevent Gracie from using momentum, Mickley counts to two before he lets Gracie push the weight off his chest.

While doing French presses, Gracie keeps his elbows close.

Mickley also watches what Gracie eats.

"After a workout, it's important for him to get a lot of protein," Mickley says. "That is one reason why I had him on an amino acid supplement for a while and eating as much protein as possible. Protein is important because it's the building blocks of your muscles."

Finally, the most important piece of the puzzle is jiu-jitsu. Gracie spends about three hours every day on the mat, turning his opponents every which way but loose. And in a matter of weeks, he'll be doing the same thing at the third Ultimate Fighting Championship.

TRAINING AT THE GRACIE ACADEMY
by Steve Neklia • Karate/Kung Fu Illustrated • December 1994

Several years ago, I noticed a magazine advertisement for a video called *Gracie Jiu-Jitsu in Action*. The ad contained a picture of several men in martial arts uniforms and a caption saying that they practiced their own unbeatable brand of jiu-jitsu. I bought the tape and was so taken with the real-life self-defense aspects of their style that I watched it over and over and showed it to all my friends.

A year later, I decided the time had come to find out more about the Gracies and their art. The first contact occurred while I was gathering information for a story introducing the major players in Brazilian jiu-jitsu (June 1994, *Karate/Kung Fu Illustrated*). Although I had been going to martial arts studios since the early 1970s and wrestling and boxing gyms before that, I was not prepared for what I would encounter at the Gracie Jiu-Jitsu Academy.

The place was beautiful, fairly new and very clean. From the reception area, I could see a juice bar and waiting area with cafe-style tables complete with napkin holders in case you had to wipe some fruit smoothie off your face. Above them, a television played most of the time, and Gracie disciples constantly fast-forwarded and rewound videotapes in search of their favorite jiu-jitsu fights. Nearby, framed covers of the world's most popular martial arts magazines adorned the wall, and every one of them sported a Gracie in action.

I walked farther down the hall and into the bathrooms. I've always thought you could tell a lot about a person or place by checking out the bathroom, and at the academy, I was not disappointed. The first thing I noticed was a wall of lockers—very important to people who work out and need to lock up their valuables. Then, out of the corner of my eye, I saw the shower area. This was the first martial arts studio with working showers I had seen, but even more impressive was the rack of fresh towels nearby. You don't even have to bring your own towel, I thought. I then discovered the reason the bathroom was immaculate: There, towel in hand, wiping down a sink, was Royce Gracie, the Ultimate Fighting Championship titleholder himself. Success hasn't changed him.

I had entered the academy with only an interview with Rorion Gracie planned, but by the time I had finished talking with him and looking around, I knew I wanted to train there. My first lesson, a free introductory class, came several weeks later. All the new students walked into a padded room where no flags hung on the walls and where a warm handshake and clap on the back replaced the traditional bow to the instructor—Rorion, in this case. As the class started, he explained that we didn't have to be strong, fast, smart or coordinated to learn his art and that it was the responsibility of the instructors to imprint this on our martial arts mentality. He said the style was developed by his father, Helio Gracie, a 140-pound man, to enable him to defeat larger, stronger opponents, and judging from the hundreds of Brazilian newspaper clippings I had seen earlier in Rorion's office, that is exactly what Helio did.

As Rorion prepared to demonstrate a ground-fighting technique, a well-built young man volunteered to be his opponent. He was told to lie on his back as Rorion mounted him—in grappling parlance, that means sitting on top of your opponent's chest with one leg on each side of his body. Rorion then told the man to try to escape. Now, I have participated in many martial arts classes—both as a student and instructor—and the norm is, when the instructor tells you to escape, you try for a while, then stop so he can show you how to do it properly. But when Rorion told the student to try to escape, he seemed to take it as a personal challenge. He gave it 150 percent, throwing punches and elbows at Rorion's head and body, and even trying to head-butt him.

The student's resistance continued for a few minutes, but Rorion just smothered his punches and elbow strikes. Every time Rorion thought he was finished and started talking to the class, the guy would start acting like a wild man again. I guess he figured that, because Rorion was not hitting or choking him, he was not in serious danger. Rorion soon caught on, and every time the student left an opening, Rorion threw a punch, stopped it a half-inch from the student's face and said "punch" just to let him know how easy it would have been.

But even this did not slow the guy. He continued to try to land blows. Just then, Lowell Anderson, a brown belt, moved forward and squatted close to the pair, then turned and winked to let us know everything was under control. After several minutes of throwing everything he had and not landing a single strike, the guy got tired and just lay there. Rorion had subdued him without ever landing a blow. I learned an important lesson: You don't have to punch, kick, choke or break a bone to subdue an aggressor. You can if you want to, but you don't have to. I guess the student learned the same lesson, for he now takes lessons at the academy.

In the locker room after class, I asked Mike Rodela, my training partner, if he also thought the student had really tried to hurt Rorion. He said he had never seen anything quite like it before. We both wasted no time signing up for class. We found out the Gracies divide their students into four groups:

beginner, intermediate, advanced and mixed (intermediate and advanced). Their system has five belts: white, blue, purple, brown and black. Because the jiu-jitsu family has been here since the early 1980s and only one black belt at the academy is not named Gracie—his name is Fabio Santos— I concluded that the Gracie Jiu-Jitsu Academy, unlike many schools that pass out belts every three months as a reward for attending class, doesn't just give away rank. Here, it can be years between promotions.

I began training the following week. Students can take as many classes per week as they want, but the staff must know in advance because a class is closed as soon as 12 people sign up. "Before, it was only private classes, one-on-one every half-hour," Royce said. "But we found out that, in a small group class, two instructors can cover 10 to 14 guys in one hour. The quality of instruction doesn't go down." I could train only once a week because driving to the academy took two hours. I felt sorry for myself because I couldn't train more—until I met a student from another state who was living in a nearby hotel while his girlfriend stayed at home taking care of the bills. The Gracies do inspire dedication in their followers.

It has now been more than four months since I started training at the academy, and every time I work out, the words of purple-belt assistant instructor Ethan Milius come to mind: "Everyone comes to the academy with their own amount of strength and quickness, but what we teach is technique. If you choose to use your strength and quickness and not learn the technique, you will leave with nothing more than you came with." I have seen Milius on the mat, and he knows what he's talking about.

THE TWO-TIME UFC CHAMP IS ALL FOCUS
by Douglas Jeffrey • Martial Arts Training • January 1995

How many words are in the dictionary? Plenty, right? You have to give *Webster's* a lot of credit. They've done the hard part by providing definitions, usages, pronunciations, capitalizations and parts of speech. You know you're going to get some comprehensive information when you look something up. The word "focus" is a perfect example.

"Focus," like many words, has different meanings. For example, it can mean "a point at which rays of light converge," or it can define "the point of origin of an earthquake." It can also mean "to concentrate attention or effort."

Certainly, no one can dispute the scientific meanings. But in all respect to *Webster's*, they missed another definition. How can you define focus without including a picture of Royce Gracie? After all, Gracie has won two Ultimate Fighting Championship titles. Is there anyone more focused?

Gracie says getting focused means many things, including training.

"When a match is coming up, it's time to train," he says. "It's time to run. It's time to lift weights. There's no skipping."

Gracie, who has won $110,000 for his two Ultimate Fighting Championship victories, says it is easy to get focused.

"I can get focused for a match in a day or less," Gracie says. "If somebody walks into our school and says he wants to fight, all I need is a second to get focused. I just assume he wants to kill me, knock me out or rip my head off my shoulders. I just turn on my switch. Everything else goes blank, and I say, 'Let's do it.'"

On the other hand, if the match is several months away, then he doesn't start thinking about the competition until a few weeks before the event.

"If a match is one year from now, I would not be thinking about my opponents," says Gracie. "When the match is about two months away, however, I am not myself anymore. I start thinking about my opponents. I eat breakfast, lunch and dinner with them on my mind. When I think about them, I really get serious, especially when I think of what they want to do to me in the ring."

Visualization

To prepare for a match, Gracie thinks about each opponent and his style. He thinks about all the techniques that style is known for, and he visualizes how he is going to defend against each attack.

"I picture the dangers each fighter will present," Gracie says. "For example, if I am going to fight a sumo wrestler, I think about all the maneuvers a sumo guy typically tries. If I am going to fight a kickboxer, I know that I should expect *muay Thai* kicks. And he will probably have good hands, like a boxer. As a result, I have to think, What if he hits me? Can I take a hit? What should I do afterward? Then I consider grappling, and I know he is done. Therefore, I will think about my timing so I can get in and take him down. It is almost like playing a chess game in my mind."

Visualizing each match helps because Gracie can plan his strategy, including several moves ahead.

"There is always a third or fourth maneuver I can try," Gracie says. "When I think about my opponents like this, it really gets me mentally prepared to fight."

Family Tradition

Thinking about his family tradition also helps Gracie get focused.

"I think about my family because they have been undefeated for so long," Gracie says. "That helps me get focused. I think, The family is undefeated. OK. I am going to carry that tradition on."

He does not, however, dwell on his family's 65-year unblemished record.

"If I totally concentrated on that, then the weight or pressure would be so heavy that I would not be able to fight," he says.

And his family makes sure he does not dwell on their success.

"My father, Helio, and my brothers do not let me think about the pressure," he says. "They make me feel like the family's success is no big deal. And they do this by never mentioning it. They never say, 'You have to win.' And they never say, 'It's OK to lose.' They do not put pressure on me."

Gracie says it also helps to have a good coach.

"I trust my dad," Gracie says. "He tells me, 'Walk straight up to him and hit him.' You have to trust him. You have to. The old man has done this so many times and for so long. He knows. He has been down that road before. When I listen to my father, I get focused."

Isolation

Keeping to himself as a match approaches is another way Gracie concentrates.

"I stay away from parties, and I stay away from crowds," he says. "I try not to talk too much or give interviews. In fact, I try not to talk too much in general, even to my friends, because that can take your focus away. People are going to tell me to be careful. Or they are going to ask me if I am ready. They will ask me if I am scared. And they will ask me if I am in shape. These questions throw you off."

It is important, however, to maintain certain contacts, he says.

"Having my fiancee around keeps me calm," Gracie says. "Things can get tense around the other fighters. With my fiancee, however, everything stays cool, especially when she gives me a hug and a kiss."

Taking Five

It's also important to take a break from jiu-jitsu once in awhile, Gracie says.

"It's important to take a break, whether it is sports or something else," he says. "You have to take a break. Look at basketball, football and baseball. Each has a season. They play and then they are off. You just can't overdo it. If you don't take some time off, you can't go any further. You can't grow."

On many occasions, Gracie has recommended that his students take some time off.

"Without a break, they start to get overloaded with information," he says. "Sometimes I will recommend that a student take a week off or even a month. When they ask me why, I say, 'Just trust me, man. It is better for you.' It always helps to take a break."

And yes, even Gracie needs some time off.

"I'll take a week off," he says. "And then it is time to come back. I have followed this routine all my life. If I don't come back by a week, however, then I start shaking. When I am like that, you don't want to sit next to me. It's a mess."

So how does the UFC champion relax?

"Surfing, running, bicycling, spending time with my girl. I am on the go all the time," Gracie says.

TEN REASONS WHY GRACIE JIU-JITSU WINS

by Joseph J. Truncale • Black Belt • February 1995

You have been a martial artist for more than 30 years and have earned black belts in several styles. You have practiced karate, judo and kickboxing with some of the best martial artists in the world, and you have won numerous tournament sparring titles. But in less than two minutes, you are choked out at a seminar by a practitioner of Gracie *jiu-jitsu*.

You think your defeat is a fluke and decide to try your luck again. But this time, the Brazilian jiu-jitsu stylist quickly applies a painful armbar and forces you to tap out in an even shorter period. Although you feel humiliated at being beaten by a person who had already fought 70 other martial artists before you, there is some consolation in the fact that each of them met the same fate as you did. Each of them was defeated by jiu-jitsu expert Rickson Gracie, widely acknowledged as the best fighter in the Gracie family. Before the seminar is over, Gracie will have humbled 100 participants, leaving each with no doubts about the effectiveness of his Brazilian jiu-jitsu.

There are many reasons why Gracie jiu-jitsu has grown in popularity in the martial arts community. The primary reason, perhaps, is the success of Rickson's younger brother, Royce Gracie, at the first two Ultimate Fighting Championship tournaments, where the latter won all seven of his matches, two championships and a reported $110,000. Martial artists, it seems have respect for any style that can consistently demonstrate its effectiveness in a no-holds-barred setting. Although some martial artists have criticized the Gracies and their system, few are willing to meet them in a full-contact match. Many people can "talk the talk," but few can "walk the walk."

Why has Gracie jiu-jitsu proved so successful in real combat situations? Following are 10 reasons for the system's effectiveness:

• A solid history. The Gracie family has been practicing and refining their jiu-jitsu system for more than 60 years. Carlos Gracie first learned *jujutsu* from a Japanese master who was touring Brazil and then taught the art to his brother Helio Gracie. The brothers eventually developed their own unique style of jiu-jitsu and taught it to their sons.

• An emphasis on grappling skills over punching and kicking. Although Gracie jiu-jitsu includes punching, striking and kicking techniques in its fighting arsenal, the system's primary focus is on grappling maneuvers. The reason for this is quite logical. The Gracies contend that most fights end up on the ground, where strikes are less effective than grappling techniques.

- A focus on safely closing the fighting distance. One of the keys to Gracie jiu-jitsu effectiveness is the practitioner's ability to see an opening and immediately close the fighting distance to clinch with the opponent. Although many stand-up fighters still believe their "deadly" kicks and punches can keep a grappler at bay, that has not been the case at the Ultimate Fighting Championship tournaments, where jiu-jitsu stylists such as Royce Gracie have been successful at avoiding such blows and initiating takedowns.
- An emphasis on choking techniques. Royce Gracie demonstrated the effectiveness of Brazilian jiu-jitsu chokes in the first two Ultimate Fighting Championship events, winning four of his seven matches via choke holds.
- Highly efficient arm locks and armbars. After chokes, the second most common Gracie jiu-jitsu technique is an arm lock, such as an armbar. What makes these techniques work so efficiently for the Gracies is that they are used to applying the locks under realistic fighting conditions. It is easy to apply an arm lock when practicing against a willing partner, but it is a much different matter when tangled with an angry opponent in a real fight. Gracie jiu-jitsu stylists, however, train realistically. Their practice sessions are like actual fights.
- Countermoves for every situation. When Helio Gracie began developing techniques that would work for individuals of any size, he analyzed in detail every move and countermove that could be done in a fight. Contrary to many of the Japanese jujutsu maneuvers, which rely on strength, Gracie jiu-jitsu emphasizes style and technique so that all sizes of practitioners could be successful.
- Techniques that work under real combat conditions. The true test of any fighting art is on the field of battle, and Gracie jiu-jitsu has certainly proved itself time and again in this arena. The Gracie system is far from a "paper tiger" art. It is geared for real fights and doesn't waste time on unrealistic prearranged fighting sequences or tournament techniques.
- Forcing opponents to fight in grappling range. Many stand-up fighters believe they can keep a Gracie jiu-jitsu stylist at a distance by using kicks, punches and other "deadly" strikes. However, experience has demonstrated that when Gracie stylists decide to move into a clinch, there is little the opponent can do to avoid it. He may score a single blow as the jiu-jitsu fighter closes the gap, but it isn't enough to stop the low-charging Gracie stylist from his objective. And once he is in grappling range, the jiu-jitsu fighter is in control and is playing his game, not his opponent's. At this range, the stand-up fighter's punches and kicks become ineffective and he is on unfamiliar ground. Game over.

- An emphasis on conditioning. As Royce Gracie's victory over Kimo Leopoldo at the UFC 3 demonstrated, the Gracies have tremendous endurance and emphasize conditioning in their training. They are willing to grab on and wait as long as it takes to subdue their opponents. At their seminars, a single Gracie instructor may grapple with 70 to 100 fresh participants, one at a time. At the aforementioned Chicago workshop, Rickson Gracie grappled for two straight hours, stopping only briefly for a drink of water. Such training builds incredible endurance.
- Complete confidence in themselves and their system. The Gracies truly believe their system is the most effective fighting art in the world. The have complete faith that their techniques will work in the pressure-packed conditions of a real fight. Unlike other martial arts, winning on the street is the primary objective of Gracie jiu-jitsu. The style's practitioners are not concerned about winning tournament titles. The fact is, punching and kicking skill alone are not enough for the realities of the street.

How, then, does one defeat a Gracie jiu-jitsu stylist? There is really only one way: You too must become an expert in the Gracie style of fighting.

That, of course, doesn't happen overnight. According to family spokesman Rorion Gracie, it takes a minimum of 10 years to earn a black belt in the system. Even a little Gracie jiu-jitsu knowledge, however, can improve a martial artist's chances in real combat situations. And if you commit yourself to 10 years of training in the Gracie system, you may have enough knowledge and experience to successfully defeat another Gracie jiu-jitsu stylist.

One thing is certain, however: It would not be an easy task.

ROYCE GRACIE SPEAKS
by Royce Gracie • Martial Arts Training • July 1995

My family has 65 years of tradition. In all those years, no one has ever lost a fight, and I don't want to be the first. I'm going to keep the flame going for another 65 years.

I think my family has been successful for a couple of reasons. First, we have good techniques. We know what to do in each situation. If you're uncertain about what to do, you're going to be in trouble.

Second, I have a lot of heart. Although some people might develop heart, I think you have to be born with it. If you're going to develop heart, you have to trust yourself and develop self-confidence. You can't be afraid.

For example, when I enter the Ultimate Fighting Championship ring, I'm not worried. If I was, I wouldn't step in the ring.

To be properly motivated, you also need some good people around you. I have my family. We are close. They make sure I'm on top of my game, ready and focused.

If I ever have trouble getting motivated, I take some time off. I don't work out. For example, if I am not up to it, I won't run. I rest and take it easy. Sometimes it's important to take the day off so you don't burn out. There are times when you might be doing too much. When I am, I take a break. And there is nothing wrong with taking a break.

Royce Gracie (top)

The same goes for jiu-jitsu. If I am tired, I take a break. It's important to pace myself so I can work out daily. If I do too much one day and get sore, it's not worth it.

It's also important to set goals. My goal is to always win the fight. I don't want to lose. That is why I train hard. And I have to be in top shape to win. And when I am facing tough opponents, I have a tendency to get

Royce Gracie (bottom)

in even better shape. These guys in the UFC can be dangerous. Yes, pride certainly motivates me. I want to be the best I can be.

To be successful and motivated, you have to like what you're doing. If you don't enjoy what you're doing, you're not going to be motivated.

Don't forget. You have to wake up each day and do the same thing again. It has to be in your blood. I love what I am doing. I can't stay away—not even for a week.

I think I enjoy *jiu-jitsu* so much because I grew up doing it. The mat was my playground. I learned to like it.

And now I enjoy teaching students. It's fun to see a beginner progress.

Your students need motivation, too. It's important to make classes fun for them. If they like the class, it makes it easier for everyone. Once they enjoy the class, it's easy. They will be like kids. They will want to come over and play. They won't be able to wait for the next class.

To make it fun, you have to provide more than just instruction. For example, the atmosphere around the school is important. If everyone is cool and hangs around, people will like it. The atmosphere should be relaxed.

You also have to treat your students right. You have to treat them like people. And once in a while, you have to throw a joke in during class.

If you're too strict, students won't want to train with you. If all they do is come in, train and go home, they won't be happy.

GRAPPLING IS LIKE SWIMMING
by John Machado • Martial Arts Training • July 1995

In many ways, grappling is like swimming in a large lake. The better you can swim, the easier you'll glide through the water. Similarly, the better you can grapple, the better you'll be able to handle yourself on the ground. And don't fool yourself. Basic grappling skills can alter the outcome of a fight.

Your grappling ability depends on your ability to trap, distribute your weight, escape from holds and apply the finishing touch on your opponent. Putting a killer finishing hold on your opponent is like "checkmate" in chess.

Once you've got the upper hand on your opponent, it's up to you if you want to inflict some damage on your opponent or let him off easy. If you want, you can really inflict some damage using *jiu-jitsu* techniques.

For example, your opponent's neck is extremely vulnerable to chokes, and you can hyperextend his elbows with an armbar. You can also apply devastating holds on your opponent's neck, elbows, shoulders and ankles, and apply spine cranks and knee locks. You can really crush some joints, if you want to.

Establish Control

When two fighters end up on the ground, one usually applies a finishing hold to end the match. Before that can happen, however, one of them has to establish control. When he gets the upper hand, he can apply the finishing hold.

The step before to the finishing hold is called the control position. You can achieve the control position from the top or bottom.

If you're on top and in your opponent's guard (between his legs), your goal is to escape without getting caught in a hold or losing your balance. When you escape, you can start the match over again.

Side Control

Once you escape, you should then try to control your opponent from the side. Side control is extremely important in wresting and judo because a pin can decide a match. In jiu-jitsu, however, you have to pin your opponent and apply a finishing hold.

There are several head locks and armbars you can apply from the side. Sometimes you can even get your opponent to submit simply by placing your weight over his solar plexus.

The Mount Position

If you can't apply a finishing hold from the side, you should mount your opponent (sit on his chest or stomach). Once you've mounted your opponent, you can apply some devastating arm locks or chokes. And don't overlook the crushing effect of elbow strikes and punches.

The ground is your ally when you throw a punch from the mounted position because it prevents the shock waves from lessening the power of the punch.

Usually when someone is on his back, he panics and turns onto his stomach; he thinks he'll be OK if he does this. This, however, is a serious mistake because he's now susceptible to chokes.

People think that nothing will happen to them just because they can't see what's going on. That's like the ostrich that sticks his head into a hole during a dangerous situation.

Both Sides of the Coin

You can't be a one-dimensional fighter. It's important to learn offense and defense. You have to learn both sides of the coin. You have to be a strong escapee and finisher. You have to feel safe and comfortable, regardless of what position you're in. Once you know how to play the grappling game from the top, you have to learn to play the grappling game from the bottom.

While it's important to learn offense and defense, you normally learn defense before you learn any finishing holds. For example, you have to learn how to escape from the mount position, which is probably more important than learning the mount itself.

If you're a nongrappler, give jiu-jitsu a try. It can really bolster your arsenal. To be sure, grappling skills make you a more versatile fighter.

The Grappling Explosion

As you probably know, grappling is exploding in the martial arts world today. And one of our goals is to keep you abreast of this progressive trend.

The more you practice, the better you'll be. And one day, you might just become the equivalent of an Olympic swimmer.

Keep training.

TOUGHEST MAN IN THE WORLD
Karate/Kung Fu Illustrated • August 1995

As well-known and respected as three-time Ultimate Fighting Championship victor Royce Gracie is, the martial arts world has heard bits and pieces about a person who, in Royce Gracie's own words, is "10 times better than me—he's the one who can beat everybody." That person is none other than Rickson Gracie, Royce's older brother.

Relatively little has been written about Rickson Gracie. He does not fight in the UFC. He does not market instructional videotapes. He does not issue challenges. Nevertheless, he is often referred to as the toughest man in the world.

Karate/Kung Fu Illustrated: Let's start with some background information. How old are you?

Rickson Gracie: I don't believe in age. I try to be ageless. I have my own understanding about time, and I think we have much more intensity if we're not concerned about age.

KKI: You are originally from Rio de Janeiro, Brazil. When did you come to the United States?

Rickson: I came to the United States a few times to do seminars, then moved to California in 1989.

KKI: When did you start *jiu-jitsu*?

Rickson: I started training even before I was conscious about training. My dad, Helio Gracie, used to play with me on the mat, so it began before I was conscious of it. That was definitely an advantage because everything you learn as a child makes you more natural. [Training] time, experience and perfect technique—it is the perfect combination.

KKI: Do you believe that a person who starts martial arts training at age 10 can ever catch up with someone who started at age 2 or 3?

Rickson: That depends. Of course, the young one will have a more natural ability to move, but there is a difference between just playing without technique and playing with perfect instruction since you were young. Sometimes when you are very young, you play around and develop bad habits about how to execute techniques. Then it's hard to fix them afterward. Sometimes a 16-year-old can learn in an ideal way and become much better.

KKI: Is it true that you have created your own fighting style?

Rickson: No, that's not true. I don't have my personal [style] because jiu-jitsu covers all the different aspects of real self-defense. The translation of jujutsu is "soft art," so that makes no restrictions on the [techniques] I can use in a fight. Once you become knowledgeable enough to really understand all the principles of jiu-jitsu, you will want to cover all the different aspects of fighting, like striking, throwing and fighting on the ground with controlling, submission holds and other stuff. The perfect fighter is the one who combines all the different skills.

KKI: Is your style of jiu-jitsu different from Royce Gracie's jiu-jitsu?

Rickson: I don't say that because we have been training in the same system. But I am one person, and he is another. Once we have a complete notion [of the art], we personalize what we do. It's the same thing done differently.

KKI: Do you call your art Gracie jiu-jitsu or Brazilian jiu-jitsu?

Rickson: I'm Rickson Gracie, I practice jiu-jitsu, and I'm from Brazil. You can think whatever you want. (laughs) I'm not too much into names; I'm more into doing it, the source it comes from, and my name.

KKI: In a real fight, is your goal always to finish with grappling?

Rickson: Not exactly because, to give an example, no matter how good Julio Cesar Chavez is as a professional boxer, he has no chance against Mike Tyson because Tyson is much more powerful. An exchange of traumatic blows is not going to be in Chavez's favor.

Hitting with my hands, knees or elbows is something I like to do when the trade is in my favor. If I get a lazy guy about my size, I'm going to try to hit him and avoid grappling. But if I have a guy with very good striking skills, it would be silly to trade blows, especially if he is 50 pounds heavier than me.

KKI: Do you always try to stay close to a bigger opponent?

Rickson: Especially if he is a striker. If he's a big, slow grappler, I will be pleased to hit him a couple of times before I get into a grappling situation. Everything depends; I adapt myself to my opponents.

KKI: When you try to adapt to a new opponent, how can you tell if he is a wrestler or kickboxer? Do you try to feel him out for a few seconds, then decide?

Rickson: I decide from the way he looks. You can see the difference between a crocodile and a bear. You are scared of both, but with a crocodile, you just climb in a tree; with a bear, you run away. I can read my opponents' intentions by the approach they have.

KKI: By whether they approach low or high?

Rickson: Yes. You can see if the guy wants to punch, kick or tackle you. The human body must position itself in a [certain] way.

KKI: Is your philosophy generally to shoot in on a guy—in which case you might not have time to judge what kind of a fighter he is—or wait for him to act before making your move?

Rickson: Sometimes I just [move] forward; sometimes I just [wait]. Nothing is for sure, especially dealing with an opponent. I like to look in his eyes. I start with the eyes, and what comes afterward is ... unconscious.

KKI: Do you maintain eye contact until you begin grappling?
Rickson: Yes, definitely.

KKI: So as long as you are punching and kicking, you look right in his eyes?
Rickson: Yes.

KKI: How do you know when to move in on your opponent and grapple?
Rickson: That is more practical than theoretical. It's hard to create a theory. It's just good timing.

KKI: In your fight with David Leveiki at the 1994 Vale Tudo in Japan, you threw a lot of punches before moving in to grapple. Did you try to distract him and wait for him to react before closing the distance?
Rickson: Yes.

KKI: So, in some situations, you just throw punches and wait for a reaction?
Rickson: Yes, because I saw him as very defensive, and I felt like punching.

KKI: But with another opponent, you might kick before going in?
Rickson: Yes. I kick a little bit, and I punch. With a guy [of Leveiki's] size, I'm looking to go to the floor.

KKI: Do you also work to develop your punching and kicking?
Rickson: Yes, but not in a professional way. I just like to play with my strikes.

KKI: Do you have any special training routine to prepare for the next Vale Tudo?

Rickson: Yes, I cut some of my classes and put more [time into] my personal training.

KKI: Do you have plans to fight in the United States?
Rickson: Probably, but nothing is definite.

KKI: Would it be in some new event set up especially for you?
Rickson: Maybe. I think the martial arts community is getting more and more interested, and more events are popping up—not just in the United States but all over the world.

KKI: Do you mean more interested in realistic martial arts events?
Rickson: Yes. It is definitely a new step in martial arts entertainment. There's no comparison between watching a fight like that and a boxing match. That kind of event is getting more popular, and more money will be involved. I'm just waiting for the right time.

KKI: Are you talking about events that allow grappling and striking?
Rickson: Yes, events that [allow] more free initiative to see who wins a match—not with too many limitations. But they are still events with a lot of sportsmanship and respect for the fundamentals of martial arts. I don't believe that to demonstrate all the potential of a fighter, an event must be without humanity or respect or be extremely violent. Events must have some way to protect the fighters and the sportsmanship because people are not there to [participate in] a street fight. A street fight is something beyond the normal sport.

KKI: Are martial arts without respect the equivalent of a street fight?
Rickson: Yes, but you cannot bring a street fight to the screen, because in a street fight, you can be dishonorable, disrespectful, cowardly or cruel, and that is not what sport or martial arts are about. Martial arts mean you can go there and fight—elbow, choke, head-butt, squeeze, throw, control—but once the fight is over, you shake hands and it's over.

KKI: Is that always easy to do?
Rickson: Yes, if you know this concept. But if a guy asks for help and then pokes your eye, bites you on the neck, pulls your hair or goes for your [groin], that's not exactly sport. I can [accept that I may] get blinded or break my neck in a fight, but I'm not going to forgive a guy if his intention is to put his finger in my eye. I've fought my whole life but never thought about biting somebody or poking somebody in the eye. Those things are totally outside of sportsmanship; you can do them on the street, though.

Although I am a professional fighter, I have much more fear of fighting a 150-pound gang member in the ghetto than fighting a 300-pound guy in competition because the guy on the street can have a knife or [get] somebody else to attack me from behind. The street fight situation is so complex. You can't just say, "Lets fight with no rules and do whatever we want to see who wins." The idea to try to represent anything-goes fighting is a little too much. I've seen a lot of violent fights, and people don't really need to get to a point where it's a personality problem or a moral problem and [they] go for a bottle or a knife. If you fight, you fight. If you lose, you just lose like a man and go home. Things must be on this level—with respect.

KKI: If you were in a tournament and your opponent bit you, would you "forget" to control yourself?

Rickson: No, I would just squeeze him a little more. But I cannot lose my control because my best friend in a fight is the technique, and the more emotionally involved I am, the less technique I apply. It's all about keeping myself focused and going a little harder when I have a chance to pay him back.

KKI: Speaking of focus, when we watch Royce Gracie in the UFC—even in a long match—he looks so relaxed and talks with his family at ringside. Does that relaxation allow him to focus on technique more clearly?

Rickson: The condition you are talking about is the perfect understanding of what's happened and what's coming. Nobody relaxes in a situation like that. You just get things under control. Emotionally you keep yourself controlled, but your mind is very intense. A lot of things pass at the same time. You never relax.

KKI: Do you relax parts of your body you are not using to conserve energy?

Rickson: Definitely.

KKI: Is that a basic principle of jiu-jitsu?

Rickson: Yes, but the most important principle is to apply leverage. That makes all the difference because the techniques are based on leverage.

KKI: How important are strength, speed and conditioning?

Rickson: For strength, speed and conditioning, much more is much better. (laughs)

KKI: But you don't need them?

Rickson: You don't need them to waste like a silly guy. But if you have them [when] you need them and combine them with techniques in the right way, it's always good.

KKI: Someone once said that, for self-defense, all you need is technique. For competition, you need strength, speed and conditioning.

Rickson: And don't forget the heart and the focus.

KKI: And experience?

Rickson: That's even better.

KKI: How do the Japanese react to having a *jujutsu* master who is a foreigner but is better than they are at their own country's martial art?

Rickson: I think they like it because they see jujutsu the way it should be—put in a very special place. Of course, I don't know if they like the fact that I'm a foreigner, but I feel like they have a very good connection with the way I am, with my philosophy, with what I know [about] the Japanese *bushido* (warrior ways). I think they like me because I bring to them the whole cultural gift and the execution of a beautiful art. They give me some kind of respect because I don't have any attitude problems and I'm a good fighter.

KKI: I heard about a possible fight between you and the Japanese UWF international champion, Nobuhiku Takada. Do you think that will happen?

Rickson: I don't think it's going to happen because it's hard for me to fight in a federation—even if it's for good money—where the fights are not 100-percent real. I am more than happy to fight Takada or anyone else—but under an independent association or promoter who can establish a realistic [event]. But I cannot put myself in a situation where, if I win, my opponent can say, "I let him win because it was his turn, but next time ..."

KKI: Because, even if the fight was not fixed, people could still think it was?

Rickson: Yes, they could say anything. So I recognize Mr. Takada's potential. I will be glad if he enters the 1995 Vale Tudo or if he wants to fight somewhere else under an independent promoter. But I cannot [risk] my reputation with an association where it's not 100 percent [real].

KKI: Does the Vale Tudo have a good reputation for real fights?

Rickson: It has an excellent reputation because the fighters fight for real. Their reputation is very good—good enough for me to be involved with because the Vale Tudo is a new event with rules specifically for the event.

KKI: Will you continue to fight in it?

Rickson: At least for this year because it's already set up. But next year ... we'll see. I like to live in the present.

KKI: What do you see in the future? Are you going to continue fighting, open schools across the country or try to get into movies?

Rickson: My intention is always to channel my energy for the present. I see a big interest in jiu-jitsu and ground fighting, and that's great. But I put my intensity [into] things I do now.

KKI: How do you deal with the growing interest in your fighting style?

Rickson: We now have schools in four places in [California:] Ventura County, West Los Angeles, Pacific Palisades and Laguna Niguel.

KKI: So you have four schools in Southern California and you do seminars, but how do you deal with martial artists in New York, Florida or even Northern California who desperately want to learn from Rickson Gracie or one of his instructors?

Rickson: I offer intensive training programs, law-enforcement training, private classes with me and regular classes in my school. The only time I don't teach personally is during the month before my fights. Fighting is something you must be focused to do.

KKI: Some people would say you have easily beaten many of the best fighters in the world. Why do you still compete?

Rickson: I don't see a relationship between having beaten some of the best fighters in the world and having to stop fighting. There's no reason to stop. If I'm the best drinker in the world, I will still drink. Or if I'm the best surfer, I'm going to [continue surfing] because I enjoy it. Jiu-jitsu is not something I need to change my personality to do. It's just a beautiful science. This science is something I'm addicted to doing, practicing, teaching and sharing with my students. I love to fight. It sounds kind of weird, but I'm not there to beat up or hurt anybody. I try to win the fight as cleanly as possible. Of course it's a dangerous sport, but so are thousands of other sports. What I try to do is use beautiful, scientific, technical maneuvers. There's nothing brutal or too aggressive about it.

KKI: Are you still learning?
Rickson: The day I stop learning is the day I die.

KKI: What are you learning: techniques, combinations or strategies?

Rickson: Jiu-jitsu is like life: You are always learning something. The foundations are one thing, but once you get to a high level, you start to develop different maneuvers to do the same movement because your opponent is improving with you. He's adapting to different ways of defending himself, so you should find ways to improve yourself. It's endless.

KKI: Some people have called you the toughest man in the world. How do you react to that title?

Rickson: I try to keep the title, eh? (laughs) I try my best to represent the science of jiu-jitsu, and I have never found anything to prove that [my] technique doesn't work. I don't think I am the toughest man in the world. It's a little silly because I'm an average person; a lot of people can run, jump and climb [better]. I find myself a guy with a lot of heart, in good physical condition, but that's not enough to make me the toughest guy. I am for sure very knowledgeable in martial arts. So far, that has kept me undefeated. It's just a [matter] of hard work and very hard searching for my own truth in what I'm doing.

KKI: If a fight continues for five or 10 minutes, what do you think about?

Rickson: I don't think; I just react.

KKI: You react to whatever your opponent does?

Rickson: Of course. I am connected with my opponent and with nothing else.

KKI: What kind of opponent gives you the hardest time in the ring?

Rickson: I don't have a hard opponent because if my opponents come on very strong in a situation, I commit myself to applying techniques away from the danger. If I have a problem, I don't know if I can handle it. So it's against my mentality to put myself in a problem [situation]. Sometimes a fight takes longer, and sometimes it takes shorter. But I try to find myself in a total understanding. It's just a matter of time—that's how I see my opponent. I don't think, "Wow! That's one fight I almost lost."

KKI: Do you mean that, as soon as you see an opponent, you prepare yourself by thinking, "It's just a matter of time. There's no question that I'm going to win. It might take a little longer, or it might take ..."

Rickson: Fights are unpredictable, and if you make one mistake, you can lose. I have the tools to handle all the possibilities I can create in my mind, so I am very confident. Based on that and my preparation to react in the right way against anything, I have the confidence I need to put myself in the line of fire. It's very dangerous, but so far, I have always done well.

IS RICKSON GRACIE THE ULTIMATE FIGHTER?
Martial Arts Training • September 1995

Rickson Gracie is 5 feet 10 inches tall, weighs 185 pounds and is built like a middle linebacker and has a record that is just as impressive as his brother Royce's. He's undefeated in more than 400 fights, which includes jiu-jitsu and sambo tournaments and Japan's Vale Tudo competition.

It's no wonder this Pacific Palisades, California, resident is so successful. Besides having an incredible amount of talent, he's got an unbelievable routine that mortal men could never handle.

—Editor

Reputation

I have been training all my life, and I am the No. 1 fighter in my family. That is not a secret, though. Royce knows that and so does everyone else.

But I think it is good that Royce is winning the Ultimate Fighting Championships and is getting that exposure. He is a good fighter. I hope he keeps getting more exposure and gets more and more famous.

Moreover, in the martial arts community, I have the reputation as being the best fighter around. And because of that, I am not only focused to keep our family tradition going but also am committed to being the best I can be.

Training Philosophy

Human beings are like machines. The better you treat your engine, the better you will respond. So I treat my engine the best I can. I am a high-performance athlete, and I need all the stamina, strength and flexibility I can get.

Strength

I don't do weights because I think they restrict my flexibility and mobility. But I need power, which is why I do a lot of solo exercises like pull-ups and push-ups. I also think it is boring to go to the gym and work out. I work out one hour each day, and I keep my heart rate above 120 the whole time.

What is my routine like? Imagine a monkey in a room. He makes a lot of different movements and plays around with different exercises. Sometimes he stands on his hands, sometimes he stands on his feet and sometimes he does pull-ups. I know it sounds crazy, but this is what I do.

During my workouts, I don't work on just strength, power, coordination or balance. I do it all at once because I need all these elements when I fight. I exercise the way I fight.

Diet

As a fighter, I have to be in perfect physical condition to train properly. If I don't feel good, I am not going to train well.

To be in top shape, you can't eat all the time. Some people snack every two or three hours, but that isn't good. Your body spends a lot of energy digesting food. If your body is constantly digesting something, you are wasting energy, which you should save for exercise.

It's important how you mix foods, too. Let's say you have a nice piece of fish, salad and brown rice. That sounds pretty good, but you can screw it up if you drink apple juice with your meal. Apple juice is great, but if you combine it incorrectly with other food, it creates a chemical imbalance in your body, which promotes fermentation and leads to other problems such as headaches, insomnia and joint problems.

I eat very light, but I get a lot of nutrients. And it works. I always have energy.

For breakfast, I have fruit. Sometimes I make fresh juice and have toast and honey. If I eat acid fruits like pineapple, I wait at least five hours before my next meal. This gives me a chance to clean my system and purify my blood.

For lunch, I might have a sandwich with avocado, sprouts and carrot juice. Sometimes I have a light meal like pasta or bean soup.

For dinner, I try to eat something heavy like chicken, potatoes and vegetables. I try to have chicken and fish several times a week.

I don't eat before I go to sleep because I don't think that is good for you. If I eat, I wait at least two hours before going to sleep.

There are certain foods that I avoid, such as pork and preservatives, and I try to limit my dairy products.

Beef? My family and I believe beef is unhealthy, but I think it is necessary. As a fighter, I think meat gives me an edge. I think the nutrients in it make me aggressive. Think about it. Every animal that eats meat is aggressive. I think it's necessary for fighters to eat meat. When I retire, I'll stop eating meat. Until then, I'll eat meat twice a month.

And of course, I don't smoke or drink.

Motivation

Of course, there are times when I feel like I can go harder and there are times when I am a little tired. For the most part, however, I am very motivated.

One reason I am able to stay motivated is because I don't put pressure on myself. For example, I don't put pressure on myself to run 10 miles in less than half-hour. I don't measure myself when I do my routine.

I adapt my routine to the way I feel. Some people like to go above and beyond their limit, but I don't think that is smart.

Fighting Strategy

I was born and raised in a family with a big tradition. We have great techniques, which is the most important difference between me and a lot of other guys.

To be a fighter, you need heart, aggressiveness, strategy and patience. When fighting, you can't just go after someone at full speed. Sometimes you have to wait for your opponent's move and counter it.

Some people think all they have to do is train hard, get strong and go forward, but this is not the approach to become the perfect fighter.

The Gracie Reputation

Our family has not lost a fight in 65 years, and I am not worried about losing now. I just focus on what I have to do, and I do my best.

We've been successful because our techniques are so effective. My dad developed these techniques, and they are the key to everything. Although my dad, Helio, is skinny and weak, he is a tough guy. He created a system that enables the small guy to defend himself.

So it's not a miracle that we're undefeated. This art gives us the tools to be undefeated. And if something does happen, it is in the hands of the gods. After all, we are human and we can make mistakes.

Jiu-Jitsu

When I am teaching, I spend eight hours a day on the mat. When I am training for competition, I spend four or five hours a day practicing *jiu-jitsu*.

Jiu-jitsu is very pleasurable. It is smooth like dancing or surfing. The techniques just flow from one to the other. The beauty of this goes on forever. I never get tired of it. My dad is 83 and he still trains almost daily, so you know it's enjoyable.

Age

In our society, people label others and themselves by their age, but I think that is wrong. I believe we have the power to be ageless. You are what you believe.

I don't worry about my age, so my mind and system work forward. I don't worry that I was younger yesterday or that I'll be older tomorrow. My focus is on today.

You can't think that you are too old for this or unable to do that. If you want to do something, you can do it. I never block myself from doing something. Even my dad, who is old, can go to the beach and swim or surf; he can do it. Of course, he has physical limitations, but he does not have any mental limitations.

Don't label yourself; it makes you age.

Future

Things are getting better for me, and Gracie jiu-jitsu is getting more exposure. I don't, however, have any plans to compete in the Ultimate Fighting Championship. Royce has handled that very well, and he is doing great.

And I hope, with the blessing of God, that I will keep defending the family tradition.

ROYCE ON OVERTRAINING
Photo by Rick Hustead • Martial Arts Training • March 1996

To get to the top, you have to beat the best. And that's why everyone wants a piece of Royce Gracie, the three-time Ultimate Fighting Champion titleholder.

Why do they think they can beat him?

Maybe it's because he doesn't weigh 275 pounds or throw vicious kicks or punches.

Why hasn't anyone beaten him?

Maybe it's because of his tremendous talent, extraordinary stamina or flawless technique.

Will anyone ever beat him?

Who knows? It may take a miracle.

This man not only is driven by an intense desire to succeed but also is determined to keep his family's 65-year unbeaten streak intact.

Believe it or not, Gracie has days, albeit few, when he doesn't feel invincible. There are days when he feels like he's running on three cylinders. Maybe he's human after all. But like a true champion, Gracie works through those off days. Here's how:

Martial Arts Training: How much time do you devote to training?

Royce Gracie: It's a constant thing. I keep the sword clean and sharp all the time.

MAT: What is a typical day like for you?

Royce: I get to the academy about 9 a.m. and spar until 10 or 10:30. After that, I do some light sparring until noon. When I'm done, I go to the gym and lift weights. I mostly lift for endurance and stamina, but I also lift for power. Occasionally, I jump in the pool and go for a swim. I don't swim for any set time or distance; I just swim until my body feels comfortable. Other times, I run on the soft sand for a couple of miles.

When I'm done, I go home, eat lunch, sleep and get back to the academy at about 5 p.m. I do some light sparring for about an hour, then work out from about 6 to 7 pretty hard. My day is done at 9 p.m.

MAT: Have you ever overtrained?

Royce: No, not really. I never get to that point.

MAT: How do you keep from overtraining?

Royce: I keep my own pace. When I run, I am not trying to beat any specific time. I am not playing against a clock. I don't have to beat my record every day. I am not doing that. I am doing my own thing. I do my own time. Sure, sometimes I work out a little slower, but other times I work out a little faster. It depends on how I feel.

MAT: Is that the key?

Royce: Yes. Yes. Definitely. That is why you have to be careful if you have a trainer. He may really push you, but he also has to know when to slow down. You might have to say, "Hey, man. I'm exhausted today." Otherwise, you're going to overtrain. That is why I don't have anyone clocking me when I run. I monitor my own time. I decide beforehand how long I am going to run. I am never pressured to equal or beat a specific time. If I had a trainer who said I had to beat a certain time, I would kill myself to beat that time. And the next day, I'd do the same thing. No. That isn't any good.

MAT: So you prefer to train alone?

Royce: When I work on my cardiovascular system, yes. If I do work out with someone, I don't worry about what he is thinking. Some guys might think, "Royce is going slow today." I am not concerned about that. I am going to keep my own pace. I am going to do my own thing. We can go together, but I am not going to keep your pace, and I am not asking you to keep my pace.

MAT: Do you use the same philosophy in *jiu-jitsu*?

Royce: Yes. I spar as hard as I feel like sparring. If I don't feel 100 percent, I take it a little slower.

MAT: Do you ever have two days in a row like that?

Royce: Oh, yeah. When that happens, I figure I have been pushing too much. I figure maybe it is time to take a little break.

MAT: How long is the break?

Royce: It depends. Missing one day of training is not going to kill you. It's not like you're going to lose a fight because you did not train on one Wednesday. If you're not feeling good, you're not feeling good. If you're sick, you're sick. There is nothing you can do. Slow down. Take a day off. No problem. Relax and come back stronger the next day.

MAT: Is that how you handle weight training?

Royce: Lifting is different. If I don't feel up to it, I lift lighter. But I always hit the weights.

MAT: When you were preparing for the Ultimate Fighting Championship, did you have days when you weren't motivated?

Royce: Yes. And when that happened, I just skipped my workout. If you try to keep going [when you're tired or hurt], your problems will snowball. It's better to take a day off and come back strong the next day.

MAT: Are we going to see you in another UFC?

Royce: Maybe next year. But I am definitely not going to enter one this year. If I don't compete here, maybe I'll compete in another country. I don't have anything lined up yet. Everyone will know as soon as I get a date.

Royce Gracie

MAT: A lot of people are going to be disappointed you aren't going to be in UFC 8.

Royce: I already beat [Dan] Severn. I beat [Keith] Hackney. I have not fought Oleg [Taktarov], but he lost to Severn. Anyway, I beat most of these guys already. And if I did not beat them, they lost to someone I did beat. So why should I bother entering, especially when they are putting a time limit on the matches?

MAT: You're particularly concerned about the time limit they've imposed, right?

Royce: Yes. My opponents know there is a time limit, and they know they cannot beat me. Therefore, they will play against the clock. When the clock runs out, they will say, "Yes, I got a draw with Royce Gracie, and he is no big deal." They will take that as a victory. For them, that is good. For me, it is not good to draw. There is no time on my fights.

If there is going to be a time limit, let me fight somebody who weighs 120 pounds, 130 pounds, 150 pounds or 175 pounds. These guys (fighters) are much bigger than me. I sure don't see anyone entering who is 50 pounds lighter than me. It's a joke. Most of those guys weigh more than 220 or 250 pounds. I am 175. Forget it. Get rid of the time limit, and we'll talk. The next thing they are going to say is you can't execute chokes or armbars. Give me a break.

MAT: It doesn't sound like we're going to see you in the UFC at all.

Royce: Until they change that rule, I won't be back in the UFC. That's right. Furthermore, why should I fight in the elimination rounds? Until they come up with some better rules or a better offer, I won't compete.

MAT: Are you missing the competition?

Royce: Yes. I miss it. I am used to being there. It is the atmosphere.

STREET JIU-JITSU VS. SPORT JIU-JITSU
by Marx Acosta-Rubio • Black Belt • March 1997

There are three major differences between *jiu-jitsu* as it is used in a street fight, and jiu-jitsu as it appears in a tournament. First, although a jiu-jitsu stylist would wear a *gi* in a tournament, he will not be so attired on the street and is therefore forced to adapt to his opponent. The opposite is true in jiu-jitsu tournaments, in which competitors rely heavily on using the gi to defeat their opponents.

Second, on the street, jiu-jitsu practitioners can punch and kick their opponents but must also avoid being hit and kicked. They don't have to worry about either consideration in tournament jiu-jitsu.

Third, the training methods differ, depending on whether you are using jiu-jitsu for self-defense or tournament competition. Those training for street defense practice under real conditions, taking in various considerations, such as terrain, clothing and weather. Jiu-jitsu competitors, however, gear their training to winning tournaments on a soft mat, under predictable indoor conditions.

The gi—both the opponent's and his own—plays an integral role in the jiu-jitsu competitor's strategy. He uses the gi for positioning as well as finishing holds. By grabbing his adversary's uniform, the tournament competitor can better control him. He will often grab the opponent's gi to initiate a takedown, then use the uniform to make it harder for his foe to move while he maneuvers for superior position, such as a mounting tactic. The jiu-jitsu competitor will even use his own gi (or his opponent's) to apply a finishing hold such as an armbar or a choke.

Few people, of course, wear gi on the street, and the jiu-jitsu stylist must find other means to approach and take down an opponent in such an environment. He will most likely attempt a double-leg takedown, which does not require use of the opponent's clothing. After the takedown, the jiu-jitsu stylist will stay close and attempt to control his opponent's limbs to avoid being hit. After establishing a superior position, the jiu-jitsu practitioner will complete his defense by applying the appropriate submission hold for the circumstances.

In tournament jiu-jitsu, the competitors are only concerned with scoring points so they can win the match. They do not worry about being hit or kicked by their opponent because those tactics are against the rules. They can score points in several ways: via takedowns, by escaping the opponent's guard, by mounting their adversary, etc. Even if they don't force their opponent to submit, they can win a match simply by accumulating the most points.

Although the street jiu-jitsu fighter must pay heed to his opponent's punches and kicks, he can deliver similar attacks of his own that are not allowed in jiu-jitsu tournaments. He can also capitalize on his opponent's strikes and kicks because such techniques often leave the latter vulnerable to a jiu-jitsu technique. There are no rules or time limits on the street, and the jiu-jitsu stylist must quickly attempt to position himself for a defense or finishing technique. There is only one way to win on the street: by forcing your adversary to submit. The victor is the person who can walk away afterward.

Training approaches also differ for tournament and self-defense jiu-jitsu practitioners. Because the tournament fighter is only concerned with winning a match, he will learn a technique, practice it and then try to apply it in "free training" (the jiu-jitsu equivalent of sparring) against a practice partner. Free-training sessions generally continue until one partner taps out, signaling he has surrendered. Sometimes, however, the instructor will designate a time limit and, if both opponents are of similar skill, the session will continue without a winner until time expires. The major focus of tournament jiu-jitsu training is not technique drills but free training, which conditions the jiu-jitsu competitor and leaves him ready for a match.

Conversely, the jiu-jitsu practitioner interested solely in self-defense has a completely different outlook on training. His desire is to quickly finish his attacker by any means possible. He therefore focuses his training on takedowns and grappling techniques such as chokes and arm and leg locks. Many times, he will cross-train in self-defense systems that include punching and kicking techniques to add some striking methods to his repertoire and thus help set up his takedown maneuvers. He will also frequently include a degree of contact in his sparring sessions to give him a realistic feel of a street fight.

What if a jiu-jitsu practitioner wants to be skilled as both a tournament competitor and a street fighter? Actually, the two methods of training and fighting are quite compatible. The jiu-jitsu practitioner need only understand the differences between the two and train with both in mind. He must realize that his first priority in learning jiu-jitsu is to be able to apply it to a real-life situation. He must train with the idea that he might one day have to overcome a 250-pound attacker high on PCP. The jiu-jitsu practitioner can always later adapt his skills to the rules of tournament competition. The biggest adjustment he will have to make is learning how to use the gi to his advantage in tournaments. By using his uniform or his opponent's to initiate locks and holds, the jiu-jitsu fighter does not have to rely on strength or any other variable but on his technique to defeat his opponent.

Jiu-jitsu competitors should bear in mind that tournaments were developed primarily to allow practitioners to test their skills in a reasonably realistic setting without the high risk of injury that comes with an actual street fight. In essence, tournament competition prepares them to defend themselves in a real fight outside the ring. By shedding the gi and training with light contact on occasion, they can further enhance their street-fighting preparedness. A good jiu-jitsu fighter is as skilled fighting without a gi as he is fighting with one. It behooves all jiu-jitsu practitioners to know how to effectively apply techniques in both situations.

WHO'S WHO IN GRACIE JIU-JITSU?

by Andre Alex Lima • Photos by Rick Hustead • Black Belt • April 1997

You can't pick up a martial arts magazine these days without coming across the name "Gracie." In just a few short years since arriving in the United States from Brazil, members of the Gracie family have established themselves as leading experts in the art of Brazilian *jiu-jitsu*. Readers were first introduced to family patriarch Helio Gracie and his three sons, Rorion, Royce and Rickson. But soon, a whole new group of Gracies arrived on American shores and began plying their trade as well. There were cousins and nephews and uncles ... Renzo, Ralph, Cesar, Carlson Sr. and Carlson Jr. There were even individuals calling themselves Gracies who were, in fact, not Gracie family members at all. Suddenly, it became confusing indeed to tell one Gracie from another.

What follows is a chronicling of some of the major martial arts players in the family, giving readers a better understanding of who's who among the Gracies:

Carlos Gracie—A son of Gastao Gracie, he holds the family record with 21 children from three different marriages. The first names of nearly all of his children begin with the letters "R," "K" or "C" because he believed they had a certain magical power and were "strong" letters. He also created and introduced to other family members a special diet—called the "Gracie diet"—consisting of natural products such as fruits and vegetables. He died in Rio de Janeiro, Brazil, in 1994 at age 92.

Helio Gracie—Born October 1, 1912, he is the current patriarch of the Gracie clan and is responsible for transforming the Japanese *jujutsu* taught by Esai Maeda into the Brazilian jiu-jitsu taught today by Gracie family members. Helio based all the techniques on leverage instead of power because he is a relatively small man. He is also noted for winning countless challenge matches, one of which went on nonstop for nearly four hours. Helio, who still teaches jiu-jitsu seminars and gives demonstrations in his hometown of Rio de Janeiro, fathered nine children.

Carlson Gracie Sr.—A son of Carlos Gracie, Carlson was considered the best fighter in the family during the 1960s and was undefeated in numerous no-holds-barred challenges. He currently owns one of the largest jiu-jitsu schools in Brazil and is a highly respected teacher. He has churned out a number of talented fighters, including his son, Carlson Jr., as well as Fabio Gurgel and Murilo Bustamante, all three of whom have competed in pay-per-view tournaments in the United States. Carlson Sr. moved to the United States and opened a jiu-jitsu school in Hollywood, California.

Rorion Gracie—The oldest son of Helio, Rorion is the individual most responsible for the worldwide popularization of Gracie jiu-jitsu. A talented fighter in his own right when he was younger, he has turned his talents to

Helio Gracie (Deborah Reed Brown designed the cover.)

Rorion Gracie

marketing the Gracie art and product line. He also serves as manager for his brother, Royce, who fought in five Ultimate Fighting Championship tournaments.

Rickson Gracie—Third son of Helio Gracie, Rickson is widely considered the best living fighter in the family and has won the prestigious Vale Tudo Fighting Championship in Japan numerous times. He has an invincible reputation in Brazil, where he has participated in countless jiu-jitsu matches, no-rules bouts and street fights.

Royce Gracie—Sixth son of Helio Gracie, Royce is the best-known family member in the United States thanks to his unprecedented three Ultimate Fighting Championship titles. He currently teaches jiu-jitsu at his brother Rorion's academy in Torrance, California, and also conducts jiu-jitsu seminars throughout the United States.

Robson Gracie—Second son of Carlos Gracie, Robson is a talented fighter and is president of the Rio de Janeiro Jiu-Jitsu Federation. Robson has three sons—Renzo, Ralph and Ryan—all of whom are skilled fighters in their own right.

Renzo Gracie—Second son of Robson Gracie, Renzo has demonstrated his jiu-jitsu skills by winning the World Combat Championship title and a superfight at the Reality Superfighting tournament in the last two years. He is also a Brazilian *vale tudo* and jiu-jitsu champion. He recently relocated from Brazil to New York, where he teaches martial arts.

Ralph Gracie—Third son of Robson Gracie, Ralph is undefeated in Extreme Fighting tournament competition. Nicknamed the "Pit Bull," he runs a jiu-jitsu school in San Francisco.

Ryan Gracie—Fourth son of Robson Gracie, he currently teaches jiu-jitsu at his school in Sao Paulo, Brazil.

Reylson Gracie—Fourth son in the Carlos Gracie line, Reylson is noted for his business acumen and has two schools, one in Rio de Janeiro and one in Northern California, where he is assisted by his black-belt sons Rodrigo and Cesar.

Carley Gracie—Carlos Gracie's sixth son, Carley was the first family member to bring Gracie jiu-jitsu to the United States. He taught the system in Miami from 1967 to 1979, then moved to San Francisco to teach.

Rolls Gracie—The seventh son of Carlos Gracie is considered by many the family's best fighter of all time, but his career was cut short when he died in a hang-gliding accident in Rio de Janeiro.

Carlos Gracie Jr.—Carlos Gracie's 10th son is the current president of Brazil's National Jiu-Jitsu Federation and the World Brazilian Jiu-Jitsu Federation. He is also an excellent instructor and operates a successful school in Rio de Janeiro.

Karla Gracie—The seventh daughter of Carlos Gracie Sr. holds the distinction of being the first female family member to reach black-belt level in jiu-jitsu.

Crolin Gracie—The 11th son of Carlos Gracie Sr. teaches jiu-jitsu in Curitiba, Brazil.

Rilion Gracie—The 12th son from the Carlos Gracie Sr. line, Rilion is an outstanding fighter and has won many competitions in the late 1970s. He runs a school with his brother, Crolin, in southern Brazil.

Gastao Gracie Jr.—A son of Gastao Gracie Sr., he fathered one son, Gastaozinho, who teaches jiu-jitsu in Brazil.

Jorge Gracie—Nicknamed "Gato Ruivo" (red-haired cat), he too was a son of Gastao Gracie Sr. Jorge was a short man who weighed just 125 pounds yet possessed spectacular technique and confronted many bigger, stronger opponents during the 1940s and 1950s. He would teach jiu-jitsu in one city until his students reached a skilled level, then would pack up and move to another city and repeat the process with a new group of students. He fathered one daughter and died in 1991.

Relson Gracie—Helio Gracie's second son, he teaches jiu-jitsu in Hawaii, where he has fought and won a number of challenge matches to prove the efficacy of the family system.

Rolker Gracie—Fourth son of Helio Gracie, he teaches jiu-jitsu in Brazil.

Royler Gracie—A national jiu-jitsu champion in Brazil and the fifth son of Helio Gracie, Royler owns a school in Rio de Janeiro and has won several no-rules challenge matches.

MODIFYING BRAZILIAN JIU-JITSU FOR VALE TUDO
by Robert W. Young • Black Belt • February 1998

After the recent losses that practitioners of Brazilian *jiu-jitsu* have experienced in mixed-martial arts events like the Ultimate Fighting Championship, a lot of people are beginning to think the art isn't all it was cracked up to be. They're saying that whenever a practitioner relies on only locks and chokes, he neglects a very important weapon—striking. They're also saying that Brazilian jiu-jitsu loses some 70 percent of its techniques when it's practiced without a *gi* (uniform).

Well, those naysayers would seem to be basing their assessments on some widespread misconceptions, says Pedro Carvalho, a Brazilian jiu-jitsu instructor based in Rancho Cucamonga, California. He says that in Brazil, there exists a form of competition called *vale tudo*, which means "anything goes." It started as a kind of personal grudge match, but now the contests are held in a ring and a referee is present. Locks, throws, chokes, kicks and punches are all permitted, and no uniforms are worn. Yet Brazilian jiu-jitsu is doing just fine there.

It's the open-ended nature of jiu-jitsu that allows room for incorporating such diverse techniques, Carvalho says. His frequent training trips to Rio de Janeiro, Brazil, are the key to picking up the most up-to-date and effective grappling-striking combinations that can be used in a no-holds-barred fight—whether it takes place in the octagon or on the street.

The Facts

"Let me explain why we train primarily with a gi," Carvalho says. "When an instructor trains a new student, he uses a gi because without it, things are a lot harder. You have to be familiar with ground fighting with a gi before you try it standing without a gi as in vale tudo competition. It's a lot easier to learn the basics on the ground when you can grab the gi. But Brazilian jiu-jitsu is very effective with or without a gi.

"In the beginning of no-holds-barred competitions in the United States, nobody stood a chance against Brazilian jiu-jitsu. Now, almost everybody—even boxers and kickboxers—trains in it. They study the art to learn how to defend against it. That means the jiu-jitsu guys have a harder time, especially when there's a big size and weight difference."

Does being good in tournament jiu-jitsu necessarily mean a martial artist is good in vale tudo? "Not necessarily," Carvalho says. "Not everybody in Brazil learns all three aspects of jiu-jitsu: fighting with the gi, or tournament jiu-jitsu; fighting without the gi, which is vale tudo; and self-defense, in which a guy tries to punch you and you have to take him down and get away. Most instructors are not teaching all three aspects; most are teaching one or two."

And there are plenty of differences involved. "When tournament guys who are used to wearing a gi enter a vale tudo competition, they feel a little lost," Carvalho says. "A lot of techniques don't work well when you're sweaty. For example, with a gi you're taught to go for an armbar when you're in the mount position. Without a gi, you shouldn't because you and your opponent are too slippery. You should concentrate on staying in the top position and trying to finish the guy with a choke or knockout."

The following five sequences, derived from basic Brazilian jiu-jitsu techniques, have been battle-tested in Brazil's vale tudo arena. All incorporate simple strikes, and none depend on you or your opponent wearing a gi.

Sequence No. 1

Start in the mount position, from which you can punch your opponent at will. Of course, he'll try to protect his face with his hands and arms. "As soon as he does that, you must get his left arm out of the way by pushing it across his neck," Carvalho says. "Then you put your head down to hold it there and circle your left arm under his neck. Your left hand grabs your right biceps. Your right hand goes on the back of your neck. When you apply the pressure, it can cut off his blood and air supply."

If the choke does not work, you can let go with your right arm while continuing to pin his left arm against his neck. That frees your right arm to pummel his unprotected rib area. After a little softening up, hop over his torso and choke him from a different angle.

Sequence No. 2

Again, you have mounted your opponent and are trying to punch him. One of his defensive options is to wrap his arms around your lower back and pull his head close to your chest. That leaves only the top of his head open to your downward-angled blows, and it would take only one or two of those to break the smaller bones in your hands. If you wish to continue striking, try using an elbow strike to the back of his neck, Carvalho says.

"Some people can take a lot of punishment from this position and still not give up," he says. That hugging position, which your opponent thinks is safe, offers you the chance to take him by surprise and perform a quick submission.

Lean forward and position your right arm so your armpit is behind your opponent's head. Then maneuver the same arm until it hooks high on his left

Sequence No. 1: From the mount, Pedro Carvalho forces his opponent to block his punches (1). He then pushes one arm to the side and slips his free arm around the opponent's neck (2). If the choke does not work (3), Carvalho can safely blast away at the ribs while keeping the arm trapped (4). He finishes with a choke executed from the side (5).

arm. Make sure your right palm is flat on the mat. Next, abandon the mount by moving your body off to his right side. "Spread your legs for balance and keep your body straight up," Carvalho says.

It's important to maintain control of his right arm, which should still be wrapped around your waist. Grasping the wrist ensures that it won't be yanked away. As you lean backward, apply pressure on his neck. "Be care-

Sequence No. 2: After achieving the mount, Pedro Carvalho again uses punches to make his opponent react (1). To avoid blows, the opponent hugs the *jiu-jitsu* stylist's torso (2). Carvalho then circles his arm behind the opponent's neck and under his arm (3). To finish, he moves to the side and puts pressure on the neck (4).

ful because if you go all the way, you can break the guy's neck," Carvalho says. "Always go slow so he has a chance to tap."

Sequence No. 3

If you have your opponent's back and are trying for a choke, he may be at a loss for an escape. When he starts getting desperate, he may try to get out of the hold by putting his right arm under your right leg so he can sneak out that way. That's when you need to place your left foot on his left hip and push so your hips move higher on his body. "Your right leg bends around his neck, and your left hand grabs your left ankle," Carvalho says. "Pull your ankle so you can hook it behind your left knee."

In a position that is really a reversed version of judo's *sankaku jime*, or

THE ULTIMATE GUIDE TO BRAZILIAN JIU-JITSU

triangle choke, you have your opponent's neck and arm trapped between your legs. "When he raises his arm, you trap that, too," Carvalho says. You can even secure it by jamming it under your left armpit.

"At this point, you can strike him with your elbow," he says. "Or you

Sequence No. 3: With his opponent held in his guard, Pedro Carvalho traps one arm and blocks punches with the other (1). He quickly encircles his neck (2), then locks his legs and executes a choke (3). If the choke fails, the *jiu-jitsu* stylist starts moving to the opponent's back (4) and unloads a few elbow strikes to the head (5).

97

can use one of several finishing techniques: You can lock his trapped arm until he taps, you can just sit forward and choke him out, or you can lie backward and push his head forward with both your arms."

Sequence No. 4

Another position in which you might find yourself in a grappling encounter is the bottom of a side head lock. While this might have presented a problem when you roamed the elementary school playground, it's not too serious for anyone trained in Brazilian jiu-jitsu or vale tudo-style competition.

The first thing you should do is use your left forearm to push upward on your opponent's neck. Then slide your left leg over his left leg and hook it around his thigh if you can. This action provides the anchor with which you will move your body to his back.

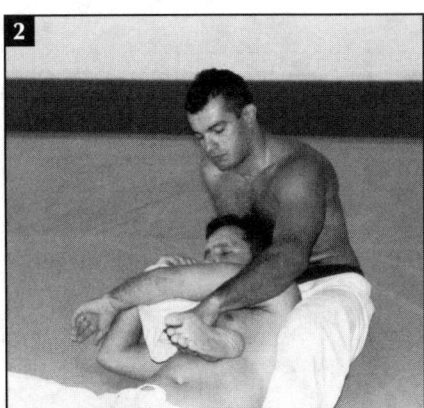

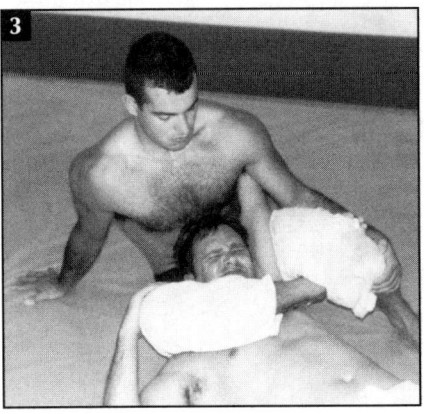

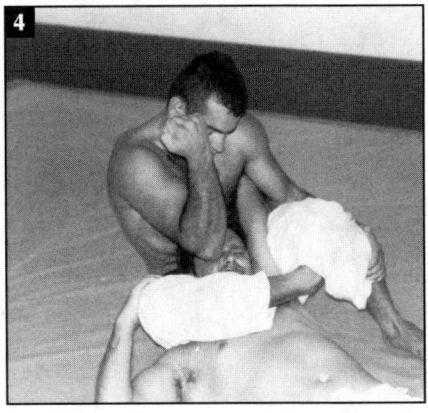

Sequence No. 4: Pedro Carvalho attempts a rear-naked choke and his opponent tries to escape by reaching under Carvalho's leg (1). Carvalho moves toward the opponent's head and wraps his leg around his neck (2). He then executes a reverse triangle choke with an armbar (3). At the same time, he delivers an elbow strike to the face (4).

THE ULTIMATE GUIDE TO BRAZILIAN JIU-JITSU

Once you're on top of your opponent, place your palms on the mat and use your left elbow to pin his head down. Then complete the transition to the mount. If you want, you can deliver a few punches to the exposed ribs on his right side. The finishing technique involves locking down his shoulder and head with your left arm and using your neck to lift his trapped right arm. Because you have secured your base on top of his body, he cannot roll out of the hold.

Sequence No. 5

Once again, you have your opponent in your guard. He tries to punch you while he's between your legs—which happens fairly often in vale tudo and mixed-martial arts competitions. You respond by blocking the punches and grabbing his upper arms to prevent any more attacks.

Next, move your left shin to your opponent's right armpit so you can

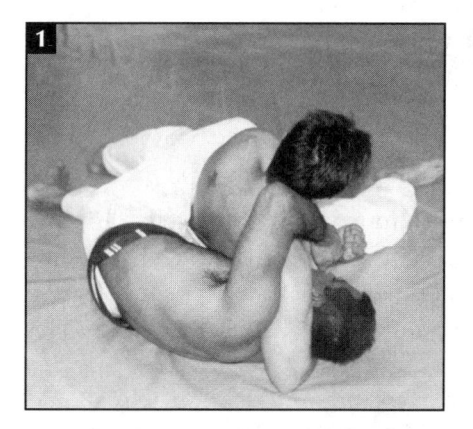

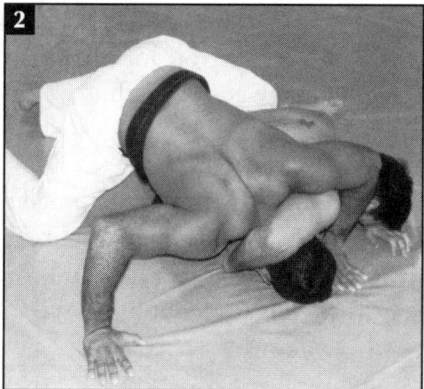

Sequence No. 5: After being caught in a side head lock, Pedro Carvalho positions his leg over his opponent's thigh and uses his arm to push against his neck (1). Carvalho then circles to the opponent's back (2). Because he maintains control of the opponent's arm and head, he can easily punch to the ribs (3). Carvalho finishes by applying upward pressure on the trapped arm (4).

push his arm away. Holding his right triceps temporarily immobilizes that limb. You then pull him toward your chest and trap his neck and left arm with your own left arm. Your head helps secure his left arm. From this position, you can choke him using the technique discussed in the first sequence.

"To finish him, you've got to get your arm against his throat and trap his arm at the same time," Carvalho says. "If he keeps his chin down, that can be very difficult to do."

If the choke fails and your opponent tries to stand and escape, maintain your grip around his neck and transfer your left foot to his right knee. "Then you push his knee to flatten him and keep him from standing," Carvalho says. "Your right foot goes over his body, and you end up on his back."

If your opponent stays flat on his stomach and you have a hard time hooking your other foot under his thigh—which will increase your stability there—you can switch to a punch or elbow strike.

"Avoid punching his head because you can break your hand," Carvalho says. "As soon as you hit his neck with your elbow, he will lift his head. Then it will be easier to choke him."

Practical Approach

For martial artists accustomed only to tournament-oriented grappling matches, the possibility of hitting and being hit can dramatically change the way you attack and defend. "Sometimes, you're in a position where you just want to defend yourself," Carvalho says. "Other times, you just want to get away.

"For example, if the guy starts to choke you or joint-lock you, why should you try to hit him?" Carvalho continues. "You should try to get out first. Then you can get in a safe position and hit him or use a finishing technique. If you try to strike when you're in danger, you might get tired. Then you'll be in more trouble, and you'll have wasted precious time."

Whenever you're in the mount, Carvalho says, you must make sure your knees are close to your opponent's armpits. "If you mount him too low, he can thrust his hips upward and throw you off," he says.

He also cautions that the guard, although an undeniably strong position in jiu-jitsu tournaments, can be bad business in a street fight. "You shouldn't put your opponent in your guard on purpose," Carvalho says. "A good jiu-jitsu fighter ends up there only if his opponent puts him there. If things go that way, there are a lot of tools that work from the guard, but you should never choose to have your back on the asphalt."

IMPROVING THE IMAGE OF THE ART
by Steve Neklia • Black Belt • May 1998

For those of you who have been living in a cave and don't know who Rickson Gracie is, here's a little background on the man. He's a son of Helio Gracie and the brother of Royce, Rorion, Relson, Rolker and Royler. He's a seventh-degree black belt, and his technique is considered to be the finest expression of Brazilian *jiu-jitsu* in the world. Most people consider him the best fighter of the Gracie clan. His innate talent and early mastery of the sport have resulted in an undefeated record after more than 450 fights, including jiu-jitsu tournaments, freestyle wrestling matches, *sambo* competitions, no-holds-barred events and street fights.

One day over lunch, I talked with Rickson Gracie about his life's goal of forming a global network of Brazilian jiu-jitsu students. He said he hopes to create a Brazilian jiu-jitsu organization as large and well organized as the judo, *taekwondo* and karate organizations.

The first step in the realization of this plan has been taken: the formation of the Rickson Gracie American Jiu-Jitsu Association. Although the association is barely a year old, it already has more than 1,500 members. To ensure a strong organization, Gracie said, he needs good instructors. He then produced a list of his "representatives," and it was chock-full of names you may recognize, including Royler Gracie in Rio de Janeiro, Brazil, Fabio Santos and Carlos Valente in San Diego, and Pedro Sauer in Salt Lake City.

Gracie's association currently has nine black belts. For Brazilian jiu-jitsu in the United States, that is very strong. Unlike in most other martial arts, there are many more potential students of Brazilian jiu-jitsu than there are qualified instructors. People want to learn but have no one to teach them. Gracie's association is trying to deal with this by sending instructors around the world to train and test practitioners of other martial arts so they can become representatives and teach Brazilian jiu-jitsu.

In case you're wondering, the first step to becoming a representative is to join the association. You can learn techniques by attending seminars or working out with a partner. When you have some technical ability and a place to teach, you can test to become an official representative.

When your Brazilian jiu-jitsu knowledge and technique reach an above-average blue-belt level, you can apply to become a "coach." Once you attain purple-belt level, you're a "training assistant." Getting to brown-belt level means you're an "assistant instructor." And at black-belt level, you're finally an "instructor."

Gracie wants the association and its students to be able to show the effectiveness of jiu-jitsu and demonstrate the benefits of sporting competition for the entire family. That's why he started organizing the International Rickson Gracie American Jiu-Jitsu Association tournaments in Los Angeles.

At most Brazilian jiu-jitsu tournaments, two things stand out. First, most competitors are young, tough guys. Second, there appears to be a lack of organization. Gracie aims to fix these shortcomings. He'll include women and children in his tournaments as soon as enough join the association, and he and his wife are striving to make the tournaments an organized, respectful affair.

Martial artists who have spent their life searching for an effective self-defense system should thank all the Gracies for transforming the lump of coal known as *jujutsu* into the diamond known as Brazilian jiu-jitsu. And they owe special thanks to Gracie for continuing to polish that diamond and making it more available to martial artists everywhere.

JIU-JITSU TRAINING IN BRAZIL
by R.A. Brown • Black Belt • July 1998

Brazil is a fascinating country, and there have always been many great reasons to visit there. The Brazilian *jiu-jitsu* revolution of the 1990s has added one more. Like everyone else, I had heard and read a lot about the Brazilian grappling art, but it wasn't until March 1997 that I decided to go to South America to see firsthand how jiu-jitsu is practiced in its motherland.

Sao Paulo

My first stop was Sao Paulo, where I met and began studying with a man named Ricardo Kowarick. He had trained under Rickson and Rorion Gracie when they lived in Brazil, and he has an extensive background that includes judo, karate, kung fu and *aikijujutsu*. In addition to his native Portuguese, Kowarick speaks Japanese well and his English is impeccable.

Kowarick's classes, like all jiu-jitsu classes in Brazil, are light on lecture and heavy on mat time. After a thorough warm-up, Kowarick would demonstrate three or four related techniques—such as an attack, a counter and a counter to the counter—then teach variations on a single maneuver or a key grappling concept.

Students would then pair off and practice the techniques. They would offer increasingly greater resistance until Kowarick sensed that they had at least a general understanding of the material. No one is expected to master every technique the first time it's presented. For that matter, no one thinks it's necessary or even possible to know every technique. (As someone in Rio de Janeiro later told me, "Jiu-jitsu is unlimited, always growing. No one knows everything, except maybe Rickson.")

The rest of the class would then be devoted to training, which in Brazil means live grappling practice, typically involving four six-minute rounds. This allowed us to try out the new techniques and practice the old ones on a variety of opponents, each with a different mix of abilities.

After hitting the mat five days a week for four weeks, I began to think that I was getting the hang of it. I was still spending too much time in the guard, but I was improving. That tends to happen when you practice every day.

But everyone kept telling me I should go to Rio. Kowarick explained that Royce Gracie's success in the first four Ultimate Fighting Championships had sparked a jiu-jitsu boom in Brazil, just as it had in the United States. Where there are Gracies, there is jiu-jitsu, he said, and until recently, most of the Gracies were in Rio.

Actually, there has always been jiu-jitsu in Rio, albeit on a much smaller scale than now. But in Sao Paulo, to say nothing of other parts of the country, jiu-jitsu is relatively new. Classes follow the same pattern everywhere, so jiu-jitsu players in Sao Paulo are becoming tough and technical. There are simply a lot fewer of them, and they haven't been doing it as long as their counterparts in the former capital. As Kowarick kept insisting, "Rio is the mecca of jiu-jitsu; if you want to see the best jiu-jitsu, go to Rio."

Rio de Janeiro

Kowarick recommended several schools in Rio. Because I had already met Rickson Gracie in Los Angeles, I decided to visit the school of his brother, Royler Gracie, first. I watched several classes and was impressed with how many black belts there were and with how relaxed their jiu-jitsu was. Royler invited me to take part in a beginner's class run by his brother, Robin Gracie.

After he taught five techniques (the *kimura*, the guillotine from the guard, two sweeps and a reversal from the *kesa gatame* head-lock position), Robin took me aside to review the basics: one way to escape the mount, one way to pass the guard, two ways to sweep (or "shave," as the Brazilians say) an opponent who tries to pass your guard, and three ways to attack from the mount. These were taught in a methodical, step-by-step fashion taken directly from the unwritten "Gracie textbook." It was familiar material to be sure, but it never hurts to review.

As I was preparing to return to Los Angeles, fate took a hand. By chance, I discovered another jiu-jitsu school, Academia de Master Jiujitsu, just around the corner from my hotel. I introduced myself to the teacher, who turned out to be Sergio "Malibu" Jardim, one of Rolls Gracie's original students who later became a student and close friend of Rolls' younger cousin, Rickson. When Jardim suggested that I stay a while longer in Rio to train, I realized I'd be crazy not to.

I started attending workouts in the morning, and generally the classes were small. Assisted by a capable purple belt named Eduardo Luna, Jardim would demonstrate three or four techniques, then watch closely as we attempted to execute them on a resisting opponent. He would stop us from time to time to comment, clarify, suggest variations and provide historical flavor. For example, after teaching the *ponteiro* choke (known as *koshi jime* in judo), he might add, "This was a favorite choke of Relson Gracie."

After class, the advanced belts were always forthcoming with helpful feedback. If I asked someone what I could have done to avoid a technique that he applied, he would offer at least one useful suggestion, if not several.

I learned as much that way as during the regular classes. Getting enough information was never a problem. To the contrary, the problem was more often simply trying to assimilate the sheer quantity of information that was freely and ungrudgingly dispensed. This free flow of facts is at least part of what has made the Brazilians so formidable. If competition makes you better, they believe, the best way to get better is to teach your training partners and students as much as they can absorb.

Competition

Jardim proved to be a treasure trove of anecdotes about the history of Brazilian jiu-jitsu, which is virtually the same as the history of the familia Gracie. He trained and grew up with the younger Gracie brothers and cousins (Royce, Royler, Renzo, Ralph and Ryan, along with Rigan Machado). Jiu-jitsu is the Gracie family's business, and every son in the family is essentially expected to begin training in the art as soon as he can walk, if not sooner. As Jardim said, "The Gracies were born in a kimono." (A kimono is what Brazilians call their gi, or training uniform).

But there are several families within the family; and they all share a common sustaining resource, which is the Gracie reputation. There is apparently some disagreement within the family as to what the ideal balance is between consuming and conserving this resource, given that each trip to the well comes with a cost: The risk of losing in a *vale tudo* (no-rules) fight with a wrestler or kickboxer, for example, and the subsequent diminution in reputation. Obviously, the more often you fight, the better your chance of eventually losing.

On the other hand, if you don't compete, you can't win. Jardim recently emerged from a 10-year retirement and competed in 11 tournaments over the past year. Two times he placed second, and nine times he placed first. Not a bad comeback performance! The key to winning or just getting good, he said, is to train smart. If you don't use your mind, he insisted, you will never be good at jiu-jitsu. The key is not how many techniques you know, because purple belts know essentially the same techniques as black belts. Rather, it is how tight you keep your game. In this sense, jiu-jitsu really is a "way of life."

Realities

Jiu-jitsu lessons in Brazil cost about $90 a month. This is a lot of money there, where roughly 87 out of every 100 people belong to the lower class and have a median monthly income of about $200. Anyone who can afford jiu-jitsu lessons, therefore, is probably a member of the small middle or even smaller upper class. These students are relatively well-educated and can often speak English.

Like most of the jiu-jitsu people I met in Sao Paulo and Rio, Jardim spoke English, and he was actually much better than he thought he was. He would sometimes ask Luna, who had studied English in California, to correct his grammar. A sample conversation would start with Jardim addressing me: "Put your arm here for avoid the choke." Then to Luna: "How you say that in good English?" Luna would reply to me, "Put your arm here for avoid the choke."

Communication was never a problem, but a little Portuguese, in addition to going a long way toward showing your sincerity, always makes it easier to understand what is being said on the mat. I often heard words like *chave* (lock), *braco* (arm) and *quadril* (hip). If I asked someone whether I correctly executed a new technique, I would hear *mais o menos* (more or less) in reply. The pronunciation can be a little tricky at first, but I got used to it quickly.

Observation is always a good teacher. One of the big benefits of training in Brazil, and in Rio in particular, is that you get to watch a lot of good jiu-jitsu players at work. One day, I observed a tournament involving the six major schools and 11 "alliances" in Rio. Most of the matches naturally were between blue belts, with substantially fewer fighters at each higher level. Blue-belt matches lasted six minutes, with four in progress concurrently. There were 10 matches between brown and black belts and only one between two black belts. While I couldn't carefully watch all four matches at all times, my vantage point was such that I was able to take in most of the action most of the time.

Matches that ended by submission invariably evoked a big reaction from spectators and teammates. But the overwhelming majority were won on points, most frequently when one fighter reversed or swept the other (two points) or passed the guard (three points). Only rarely did anyone get mounted.

As with wrestling and judo, jiu-jitsu matches begin on the feet. Most takedown attempts were of the single-leg wrestling variety, although some fighters went for a double-leg *baiana* takedown. The most successful takedown would happen when one fighter simply jumped up and put his opponent in the guard while he was still standing. Players who attempted this first seldom failed; hence they were able to begin floor fighting from the almost universally preferred guard-bottom position.

Very few judo throws were attempted, and even fewer succeeded. Even though judo throws don't seem to work very well in jiu-jitsu competition, they are taught in Brazilian schools because being able to threaten with one attack makes it easier to execute another. If your opponent is neglecting to defend a particular line of attack, that is precisely where you should attack. You must keep in mind, however, that he may be deliberately setting you up for a counterattack. Maneuvering him into an indefensible position is one way to win in jiu-jitsu, making it similar to chess. The difference is that in chess, you don't get choked out.

In nine of the 10 matches between brown-belt and black-belt players, the brown belts won. Jardim assured me that this outcome was anomalous. He believed that in this instance, the brown belts were close to promotion and simply wanted to win more because in Brazil, beating a black belt is one of the things you need to do to become a black belt yourself. And as Jardim said, "Everybody wants that *faixa preta* (black belt)." He also mentioned that the black belts in the tournament were fairly fresh and had not competed much since getting promoted.

Nevertheless, the Brazilians I met struck me as being much less belt-conscious than Americans. In Sao Paulo and Rio, white belts and blue belts said they hoped to avoid promotion as long as possible. But avoiding promotion is incompatible with a second—and even more imperative—goal, which is to become more effective and more efficient on the *tatame* (mat).

These twin goals combine to inhibit "belt-flation." In jiu-jitsu, belts represent what you can do in a competitive situation, not how many classes you have attended or how many techniques you know. There are no belt tests. In a sense, you are tested every time you train. The goal of training is sometimes simply to maintain or escape a particular position, but more often it is to "finalize" your partner, who is resisting vigorously.

Being finalized by someone at your own belt level is just one of those things that sometimes happen, but submitting to a lower belt is embarrassing, even humiliating. No one wants a belt that doesn't "fit," as the Brazilians say, and there is only one place and one way to prove that it does fit. Whether in the United States or in Brazil, the tatame is both the laboratory and the courtroom of final appeal.

ULTIMATE WARRIOR

by Douglas Jeffrey • Karate/Kung Fu Illustrated • December 1998

Scene I. Denver. Locker room. Mammoth Event Center 1993. For the second consecutive time, Royce Gracie had just defeated every opponent he faced in the Ultimate Fighting Championship (UFC 2). I was trying to get into the locker room to interview him for *Black Belt*, but the security guard wouldn't let anyone in, including the press. I couldn't believe it. This guy wouldn't budge, so I figured I'd find another way in. And I found one.

When I wandered in, I found Royce sitting next to Rickson Gracie, his older brother. Royce was smiling from ear to ear, and he couldn't stop talking about his second flawless performance in no-holds-barred fighting.

Scene II. Charlotte, North Carolina. The hotel weight room before UFC 3. 1994.

I finally got a chance to talk to Royce, and I could tell something wasn't quite right. He was subdued. He definitely wasn't himself. Why? I'm not sure, but he said he prepared for this UFC without Rickson's help. I figured that might explain his demeanor. Sure enough, Kimo Leopoldo roughed Royce up in an early match, forcing the Brazilian to bow out of his semifinal match.

Scene III. Tulsa, Oklahoma. UFC 4 1995.

Royce defeats Dan Severn to capture his third UFC title.

Scene IV. Charlotte, North Carolina. Independence Arena. UFC 5 1995.

A bloodied and battered Royce Gracie leaves the octagon after his 36-minute draw with Ken Shamrock in the Superfight.

Scene V. Valencia, California. 1998.

Looking relaxed and happy, Royce, accompanied by his wife and son, arrives at *Black Belt* for an interview and photo shoot. We've heard all of the rumors, and we're anxious to let Royce address them. Among other things, we've heard Royce doesn't want to fight because the fighters are too big. We've also heard that Royce isn't really injured.

Well, forget the rumors. You're about to find out from the man himself exactly what's going on. Was his match with Shamrock the famous final scene? Will he fight again? Can anyone beat him? Are no-holds-barred events on the verge of extinction? Is he really hurt? Royce is going to answer all these questions and more.

Finally, after all the speculation, you're about to find out if the curtain has gone down for the final time on Royce's career. Or will the confident Brazilian make an encore that tops everything he's already accomplished?

Karate/Kung Fu Illustrated: Tell us about your injury.

Royce Gracie: It started with numbness in my fingers on my right hand. Eventually, the numbness traveled to my entire right arm and right leg. The doctors said it was a bulging disk and a pinched nerve in my back. I got an MRI scan from a specialist, and he said, "Don't fight, don't stretch and don't do anything until the numbness goes away." It's one of those injuries you have to just give time to heal. I'm not sure how the injury occurred. It could have been from running, lifting weights, walking or simply sleeping wrong. You can wake up one day and have it.

KKI: When did it start?

Royce: Late 1997. I first noticed the problem in late November and early December.

KKI: What was your initial reaction when you realized you were hurt?

Royce: I wasn't overly upset. I took it as a sign that something was wrong, and I needed time to rest. That is the way I look at it.

KKI: What is the status of your back right now?

Royce: I'm feeling OK. It's about 85 percent healed. The numbness still happens pretty regularly, though. In a couple more months, I should be recovered. Right now, however, I feel like I have duct tape on my right leg from the knee down. It isn't really numb, but it feels heavy, like I don't have that much control over it.

KKI: Have you started training?

Royce: Actually, the doctor just released me to start training again. I swim, run and work on balance to get my motion back. I can't lift weights yet, though.

KKI: If you fight again, are you concerned you may aggravate your back injury?

Royce: Not really. That doesn't even bother me.

KKI: Some people are saying that your back injury is a ploy to get out of your fight with Mark Kerr. Are you aware of that?

Royce: Yes, and that is why I want to fight Kerr first after my recovery.

KKI: So you do want to fight again?

Royce: Yes. I want to fight Kerr.

KKI: Why do you want to fight Kerr?

Royce: A couple of reasons. First, he is supposed to be one of the toughest guys around. Second, he's the one I'm scheduled to fight.

KKI: Are you going to fight in Japan?
Royce: Most likely, and it will be a PRIDE show.

KKI: Can you estimate when the fight will occur?
Royce: I'll fight Kerr six months after the numbness in my leg goes away.

KKI: What do you think about fighting Kerr?
Royce: He is a big, strong wrestler. That is all to his advantage. I'll have to find out what kind of problems he can give me.

KKI: Will his strength work to his advantage? Will it cause any problems for you?
Royce: It could be a problem for me, but I'm used to dealing with people who are bigger and stronger than I am. Everyone is bigger than me.

KKI: Do you still watch the UFC?
Royce: I try to, but it's hard because the people at home don't really care. If I'm out of town, I'll watch it at somebody's house. If I'm in town, I get together with some of the students. It is good to keep in touch and see who is fighting and what they are doing.

KKI: Have you seen all the UFCs since you last fought?
Royce: Yes.

KKI: What do you think?
Royce: The big, strong competitors are not martial artists. It is almost like the UFC competitors don't have much of a martial arts background anymore. What they do have, however, is a good appearance for television.

KKI: Do you like the weight divisions and the new rules the UFC has implemented?
Royce: I don't like the rule changes. I prefer the matches with no time limits. That is the main thing I don't like. If they had weight divisions when I fought, I would have fought as a heavyweight, although I would have been a lightweight. The whole idea of this contest is to see who has the best technique.

KKI: Do you think the UFC will survive, or is it doomed?
Royce: They are slowly losing their fire, but what can they do to survive? They could change the rules again, but that doesn't even seem to satisfy the cable companies, the politicians or the boxing commission. A lot of people are trying to ban it.

KKI: Some suggest that the boxing community is trying to shut the UFC down because they are taking away some of their viewers. Do you think

there is any credibility in that?
Royce: Yes.

KKI: Let's look at the UFC and no-holds-barred fighting from another perspective. The traditionalists in the martial arts think that the UFC and NHB fighting is not really good for the martial arts. What is your reaction?

Royce: There is only one way to find out which style is the best and what techniques really work. And that is no-holds-barred fighting. Which

PHOTO BY RICK HUSTEAD

Royce Gracie

moves and what takedowns are really going to work when your opponent is fighting back? There is only one way to find out. If you think the karate guy will do better, do it. Put the kickboxer up against the karate guy and see which style is the best. It is very easy to talk about it. But get a good kickboxer and a good karate guy and put them together. Then we'll see.

KKI: I suppose the death of Douglas Dedge in a Russian no-holds-barred fight did not help matters any.

Royce: Actually, one of the guys who was in Dedge's corner came by the Gracie Jiu-Jitsu Academy and told us that [Dedge] had a previous heart problem. Therefore, he apparently didn't die because of the blows he took in the match. People can take more punches than he took and survive. He died because the doctors apparently didn't check him out before he went into the ring.

Nevertheless, people seem to latch onto things like that to support their opposition.

A young member of the Gracie clan performs a rear-naked choke.

The organizations who don't want no-holds-barred fighting have given it more attention than it deserves. They want to cut out no-holds-barred fighting as soon as possible.

KKI: Do you think Dedge's death hurt the no-holds-barred community?

Royce: No. People die playing football, boxing and wrestling. Regardless of what sport you're talking about, someone can get hurt. It would be impossible to stop everyone from competing.

KKI: When you compete, do you worry about getting seriously hurt?

Royce: I am somewhat concerned, and that is why I am so concerned about protecting myself; I want to get out as clean as possible. My first objective is to not get hurt. Next, I want to beat my opponent.

KKI: Do you think anything else can be done to ensure the safety of the fighters?

Royce: The fighters can stop the fight, the cornermen can stop the fight and the referee can stop the fight. Some referees are not good, and some cornermen don't throw in the towel when they should. But the good cornermen and the good referees will take care of the fighters.

KKI: Do you think UFC referee John McCarthy was breaking up the fights too soon?

Royce: There were a couple fights that he broke up too fast.

KKI: Isn't it better to be safe than sorry?

Royce: I think he broke up a couple of those fights early for two reasons. One, I think he was responding to the criticism that the event is too dangerous. Two, I think he was simply trying to protect some of the fighters. You can be too protective, though, and that is the other extreme.

KKI: Which fighter impresses you in the UFC right now?

Royce: Actually, it's hard to impress me, but they are all tough guys. Some of the fighters demonstrate good technique, but other times, it does not show because they are fighting such a poor opponent.

KKI: What do you think about Maurice Smith?

Royce: He is a good kickboxer. He thinks he knows the ground, but he doesn't. He plays a good defense. Randy Couture beat him, but Couture didn't know too much about finishing holds, either. Couture just knew how to control Smith. Couture won because he was on top. I wish they hadn't had any time limits in that fight because you couldn't see who was really going to take whom. That is the problem with the time limit.

KKI: What do you think of Frank Shamrock?

Royce: I like the finishing holds that the Lion's Den fighters use. Frank—like Ken (Frank's brother) and their other fighters—is a tough fighter.

KKI: If you fought Frank, how much trouble would he give you?

Royce: I can't say. We'll have to find out.

KKI: Could he beat you?

Royce: No. There is no way.

KKI: What do you think of Brazilian Vitor Belfort?

Royce: Vitor has a lot of skills. He is at the top of his career. He's a good boxer. However, if it goes past two rounds, which is six minutes, he is done. He doesn't have any endurance.

KKI: How about Couture?

Royce: He's a great wrestler. He knows the game, he knows when to get in the clinch and he knows when to stay on top. If he knew more finishing holds, he would be more dangerous.

KKI: What do you think about Kerr?

Royce: Same thing. The problem with wrestlers is that they are not used to the finishing holds. Wrestlers take you down to the ground and pin you and throw you. They don't know what else to do.

KKI: Do you think that David "Tank" Abbott's style is bad for the martial arts?

Royce: I wouldn't say it's bad. It is good to have a guy like Tank, a guy who is a brawler. You have to use technique to beat him. You won't beat him by just punching him. You have to set him up and use the techniques. People who try to match strength with him are going to have a tough time.

KKI: Leopoldo, whom you defeated in UFC 3, has done some ground work since you fought him. Do you think he would be a tougher opponent for you now?

Royce: I guess I changed his life, huh?

KKI: Some of the Brazilians have lost in competition recently. Do you think this has hurt Brazilian *jiu-jitsu*?

Royce: Yes. They've lost because they are playing the wrong game. They come over to fight and they start a punching and kicking game. That is not their game. They act like they don't know what to do if the fight fell to the ground. That is the problem.

KKI: When you get back in the ring, will you continue to fight in a *gi*?

PHOTO BY ROBERT W. YOUNG

Royce Gracie grapples with a young Brazilian *jiu-jitsu* enthusiast.

Royce: Yes. Why not? Let's say you and I spar. After 10 minutes, you take your gi off. What makes you think you are going to beat me then? My defense is still the same. It might get harder for me to catch you, but it isn't going to be easier for you to catch me. My offense gets more difficult, but that doesn't bother me at all.

KKI: How much of a factor does punching play in your strategy?

Royce: I don't punch somebody bigger and stronger than me. If I hit him, he'll smile, hit me back and knock me out. I do practice punching and kicking, but I am not going to depend on those techniques. I can choke an opponent, regardless of how big, small or strong he is.

KKI: What makes a good jiu-jitsu fighter?

Royce: Someone who knows jiu-jitsu and does what he knows during the fight. A good jiu-jitsu fighter knows how to use the finishing holds on the ground, how to defend himself on the bottom, and how to attack from the bottom and the top.

KKI: After winning UFC 1, 2 and 4, did anyone come to your school and challenge you?

Royce: No. In fact, most of the fighters wanted to take classes from me. They wanted to learn my style so they can give me a better fight. Somehow, that doesn't sound too good to me. You want to learn from me to give me a better fight? I don't agree with that.

KKI: What is it like when you go back to Brazil? Has the UFC increased your popularity?

Royce: Yes, but my family has been there for a long time. We have very enthusiastic sports fans in Brazil. For example, we have guys who would die for soccer. We also have guys who would die for jiu-jitsu. When they like something, they are fanatics.

KKI: What is your best UFC memory?

Royce: That would have to be UFC 4 because people thought that I was done fighting competitively and then I came back. I didn't just come back, but I beat somebody bigger than ever. That was the best one.

KKI: Do you ever watch the videos of those fights?
Royce: Yes.

KKI: What do you think of them?

Royce: UFC 4 was the best UFC of all time. There was a tremendous

Royce Gracie defends against a kick at a self-defense demo.

amount of excitement in that fight with Dan Severn. The commentators were even excited. If it was a movie, you couldn't have written a better script.

KKI: Your family has quite a fighting reputation. How many years have you guys gone undefeated?

Royce: I think it's 65 or 70 years. Something like that.

KKI: Does that create more pressure on you when you fight?

Royce: I don't think about it. I definitely don't think about it. It's a lot of pressure, but only if you think about it.

KKI: Is there anyone out there who is capable of beating you?

Royce: Besides my wife and kid? Or my sister, my dad or my mom?

KKI: What kind of training are you doing now?

Royce: The main thing now is to come back slowly. It is going to take some effort to go slowly because I'm very competitive, and I can't rush out there and get to work. I haven't worked out for a while, so my back and legs get pretty sore after I work out now. I have to slow down and pace myself. I have to come back slowly. I train one day and take the next day off.

KKI: What kind of cardio are you doing?

Royce: I ride the stationary bike. I haven't been running as much, yet. I just started again. I also walk on the beach and do jiu-jitsu. For now, that is enough.

KKI: What do you do to prepare for a fight?

Royce: When I'm getting ready to fight, I'll increase my running and rope jumping and get back on the weights. I may also cut down on the classes I teach so I can practice more.

KKI: Why do you think you have been so successful as a fighter?

Royce: I do what I know. That's it. Technique is more important than anything else. I don't depend on strength or size to beat these guys; I rely on technique.

KKI: If technique is the most important thing, why do you lift weights?

Royce: My father is against lifting weights. He never lifted weights in his life. He never even did one chin-up. So he says to me, "Why are you wasting your energy lifting weights?" I do it because it is a great way to keep your body fit and healthy. My dad only did jiu-jitsu. So he doesn't really approve when we go and lift weights and swim and exercise. We just think it is better to be fit. Besides, the competition is getting better and stronger. I am already giving them the weight advantage in the heavyweight division. I need to get used to throwing around more weight. I know I'll never be the strongest, but I'll be as strong as I can.

KKI: What would anybody have to do to beat you?

Royce: Do you really expect me to give that secret away?

KKI: How is your relationship with Rickson?

Royce: We are brothers. I would die for him. If he needs anything, he knows he can depend on me. And I can depend on him. We just are separate because of the business.

THE TREASURE KEEPER
by Steve Neklia • Martial Arts Training • May 1999

Rickson Gracie is a seventh-degree black belt, and his technique is considered the finest expression of Brazilian *jiu-jitsu* in the world. Most people believe that he is the best fighter of the Gracie clan. His innate talent and early mastery of the sport have resulted in an undefeated record after more than 450 fights, including jiu-jitsu tournaments, freestyle wrestling matches, *sambo* competitions, no-holds-barred events and street fights. In the following interview, Gracie discusses a variety of subjects, including training, nutrition, fighting strategy, honor and more.

Martial Arts Training: Your family has only lost a few times in 70 years. How much pressure does that create for you when you fight?
Rickson: Actually, the pressure is there anyway. I just try to do my best and not think about anything else.

MAT: Is there such a thing as an easy fighter?
Rickson: Not before a fight—only after.

MAT: What qualities does a successful fighter need?
Rickson: A successful fighter must have physical, mental and spiritual qualities, and he must combine them together. For example, a successful fighter must have determination, heart and skill.

MAT: Do you change your strategy when you fight a muscular fighter?
Rickson: The size of the opponent does not matter. I always adapt. If he's strong, I will adapt. If he's fast, I will adapt. If he's light, I will adapt. My strategy is to protect myself and take advantage of my opponent's mistakes.

MAT: What are your strong points?
Rickson: I think it's my endless search for the best technique in jiu-jitsu.

MAT: What are your weaknesses as a fighter?
Rickson: I don't even think about that.

MAT: In his book, *Inside the Lion's Den*, Ken Shamrock—the former Ultimate Fighting Championship Superfight winner—said he wasn't fully prepared for his second fight against Dan Severn. Have you ever gone into a fight unprepared?
Rickson: Basically, you are never 100 percent prepared. You always think you are prepared, but it's impossible to say for sure. However, it is important to believe you are.

MAT: People want to know why you don't do any instructional segments in magazines, books or videos.

Rickson: I never do jiu-jitsu for the money. Besides, when people train with me, they learn the respect, friendship and brotherhood that is involved in the art. This is something that can't be taught or felt through a video. Jiu-jitsu has always been my treasure, my family treasure. It's not that I am afraid to share my techniques, training or conditioning routine; I just want to make it special when I do teach it.

MAT: You recently defeated Nobuhiku Takada for the second time. What was different this time?

Rickson: Everything was different. For example, all the pressure was on me because Takada had nothing to lose. In addition to that, Takada was a smarter fighter this time. I don't feel he was any better technically in this fight, but he didn't make the same mistakes he made in the first fight. He did not go to the ground as easily. He tried his best to hit me while we were standing up. He tried to keep me against the ropes. I would say that Takada was much more strategically and mentally balanced in the second fight.

MAT: Some people thought you could have finished the fight much sooner than you did.

Rickson: Every fight is a new fight. Besides, Takada demonstrated better overall balance this time. Therefore, I took it slow until he made a mistake. I was being cautious because I didn't know if he had any tricks I hadn't seen. It's important to be patient and not lose focus of the victory at the end of the fight. Actually, I was prepared to fight longer if it was necessary.

MAT: What do the Japanese think of Takada?

Rickson: He is currently the most famous fighter. The big thing about fighting him is that I am limited to the martial arts community for the people who are really interested, but everybody knows Takada—from the youngest to the oldest. He's a national idol.

MAT: So he would be like a Mike Tyson here—before the biting?

Rickson: Yes, he's like Hulk Hogan or Mike Tyson.

MAT: Do they know his name from fixed wrestling matches or from real fights?

Rickson: They believe Takada is 100 percent real. Of course, he had some big fights as a pro wrestler, but the Japanese believe in Takada's skills.

MAT: Has anyone ever asked you to do a fixed fight?

Rickson: Yes. However, that's totally against my principles. I call myself only a fighter, a martial artist and a teacher. I'm definitely not an entertainer. I don't have any desire to use my skills to just entertain people by sometimes losing and sometimes winning fake fights. It's against my honor.

MAT: How do you prepare for a fight?

Rickson: I use a combination of three basic elements to prepare. I prepare mentally (strategic aspects of the fight), physically (physical and technical conditioning) and spiritually (your capacity to overcome fear). I believe I have been mentally and spiritually prepared for the last 20 years, but it takes two to three months to get in the physical shape I want to be in for a fight.

MAT: Do you visualize your fights?

Rickson: Yes. It's important to do this because you can prepare for different situations in a fight—the good and bad.

MAT: When you're getting ready for a fight, what is your diet like?

Rickson: As the fight gets closer, I add more protein to my diet. I also increase my number of meals from four or five per day to five or seven meals per day. Two days before the fight, I decrease my protein intake and increase my carbohydrate intake.

MAT: How important is nutrition in your success?

Rickson: Nutrition is everything. As you know, we are what we eat. If you eat properly, you will do well. If you eat poorly, you fight poorly.

MAT: What types of food do you typically eat?

Rickson: I like to eat all-natural, organic food. I eat a lot of protein, carbohydrates, vegetables and fruits. I eat white meat almost every day. I eat red meat maybe once every 15 days.

MAT: What type of food do you try to avoid?

Rickson: Besides canned foods, I try to stay away from pork, vinegar and heavy dressings.

MAT: Do you have other fights scheduled?

Rickson: I have had many proposals, and we are trying to put some things together with some promoters. However, due to other commitments, including my association, schools and family, I will probably fight only one time per year.

MAT: I understand that you trained quite awhile for the PRIDE fight.

Rickson: Because of the delays, I trained hard core for about six months.

I basically need about three months to get ready for a fight.

MAT: That must take a lot of time away from your teaching schedule. Does it cause any problems at your schools?

Rickson: I have instructors who run the schools by themselves when I'm not there. Of course, for me, I wonder if there is something missing in my routine. I also believe the students miss me, but my absence is a phase, and we all adapt.

MAT: When you get to such a high level in any art, is it hard to find good training partners? Obviously, you can beat any partner you have. How do you find a challenge?

Rickson: The key is to reduce your elements. This makes average opponents tougher. Therefore, the challenge is there.

MAT: Does that mean that you tell yourself, "Well, I won't do any advanced techniques that he doesn't know," or "I'll use only 50 percent of my speed"?

Rickson: Yes. There are many variations to make yourself weaker. For example, you can decide to just work from the bottom or whatever. That makes a big difference because an average guy can give you a much harder time.

MAT: How do you stay motivated?

Rickson: I think what really motivates me right now is the fact that I can use jiu-jitsu to positively influence other people.

MAT: What do you do when you have trouble getting motivated?

Rickson: Sometimes, I feel like I need a change of direction. Basically, however, I never lose motivation—I just change my focus.

MAT: Are no-holds-barred events in Japan the same as NHB events in the United States?

Rickson: There is a big difference between the events in Japan and the events in the United States. In Japan, they value the traditions of the martial arts, including respect and sportsmanship. After Royce [Gracie] left [following the third UFC], we started seeing in it and other events more of the brutal and violent aspects of martial arts. They are no longer about how you win a match; they're about how one fighter can pound another one and who can receive the most punishment. Those concepts are more sensational, and they bring a bad name to what are supposed to be very martial arts-oriented and philosophical events. They're supposed to be for people who devote their lives to the martial arts. They're supposed to be for them to test their skills, but in many cases, that isn't exactly what happens.

MAT: Why do you think NHB events and the situation surrounding them are improving in Japan while they are worsening in the United States?

Rickson: Because the Japanese are sensitive to the concept of being a martial artist. They're not interested in the brawling aspects.

MAT: Is it because Japan possesses what is called a "martial" culture?

Rickson: I think so. They cannot separate the sensational aspect of fighting from the traditional or philosophical aspect—or from *bushido*, which means "way of the warrior." So they unify everything. If a fighter has a bad attitude, if he lacks respect even though he wins—the Japanese will have a different impression of him. They watch an event in total silence, and when they see a movement, they all say "oh" at the same time. That shows that they have a connection with what's going on in a fight.

MAT: Many people are saying that if NHB events succumb to political pressure or stop making enough money to survive in the United States, they might move to Japan or Brazil. Do you think there would be any differences in the way they are organized if they were to make such a move?

Rickson: Basically, no. The Japanese and the Brazilians love to fight. They love to see action. There's an open door for this kind of event in both countries.

MAT: Are you going to fight again in the PRIDE event?
Rickson: I don't know yet.

MAT: Do you have plans to fight a big-name American fighter in Japan? Some people accuse you of fighting only mediocre Japanese fighters about whom the American public knows nothing. They say that if you fought someone like Ken Shamrock or Marco Ruas, they would have more respect for your abilities.

Rickson: I'm open to fighting anyone. It's not about me saying I want to fight this person or that person. It's about how interested the promoters are in promoting a fight like that. So I just keep on training and waiting for my next opponent.

MAT: So what the promoters work out is fine with you?
Rickson: Oh, definitely.

MAT: You have had many fights in your career. Have you had any thoughts about retiring?

Rickson: It's hard to say because, for me, fighting is a passion. It is something I do to maintain the family tradition. At some point, my body will tell me that I don't have the endurance or I suffer some kind of injury. Then I will stop. Besides, I am concentrating on today, not tomorrow. Being ready for today has made me think about the present and not worry about the future.

ATTACKS AND TRAPS FROM THE GUARD
by Ella Morse • Black Belt • December 2001

Combat has been part of Pedro Sauer's life since he was 5. That's the tender age at which he took up the sweet science of boxing. Later, he added *taekwondo* and judo to his résumé, but it was not until he had turned 15 that the Rio de Janeiro, Brazil, native experienced an epiphany: Childhood chum Rickson Gracie introduced him to his dad, Helio Gracie.

"Oh, you're a boxer," the revered founder of Gracie *jiu-jitsu* said to the boy. "Let me see how you do." The Gracie patriarch then had Sauer spar with his 8-year-old son, Royler. As the teenager expended his final ounces of energy fighting off Royler's choke, he saw the light. Recognizing the effectiveness of the grappling art, Sauer returned to the school the next day and signed up.

A self-described fanatic for the Brazilian interpretation of the Japanese art, Sauer trained seven days a week. Helio Gracie took him under his wing, and for six years, he supplemented his expanding knowledge base with private lessons from Rickson Gracie. "He was the guy who showed me everything I know," Sauer says.

After graduating from college, Sauer put in 11 years as a stockbroker in Brazil, but he eventually realized his interests lay in mutual combat, not mutual funds. He then decided to move to the United States to pursue his dream of teaching jiu-jitsu. When he relocated to California in 1990, the man who helped him obtain a green card was none other than Chuck Norris, whom Sauer had met in Brazil in 1985. Once he settled in, he lived with Rickson Gracie and trained extensively with his father, brothers and cousins.

In December 1990, Sauer moved to Utah and introduced the South American art there. He rapidly built a reputation as one of the best instructors in the United States. The 43-year-old has enjoyed such success for several reasons: He holds a fifth-degree black belt from the Federacao de Jiu-Jitsu and a third-degree from Rorion Gracie. In fact, he is the first person outside the Gracie family to earn a black belt and teach in the United States. Sauer is now striving to build up his own school, the Pedro Sauer Brazilian Jiu-Jitsu Academy in Salt Lake City. More than 2,000 students there and in 20 affiliate schools across the United States are developing under his guidance, and even more experience his wisdom in the weekly seminars he conducts across the country. In addition, he teaches elite protection units such as SWAT teams, the FBI and CIA.

"Now I'm trying to go a little bit away from Brazilian jiu-jitsu and build Sauer jiu-jitsu," he says. One thing he hopes his new system will do is inculcate students with more respect, self-confidence and self-discipline while they learn the best grappling techniques and strategies in the world. The following are five of those gems.

Deceptive Attack

One of Sauer's favorite offensive strategies is a deceptive little number he calls the double attack. It is used to set up an opponent for an armbar. Start on your back with your opponent in your closed guard. Dig your right hand in deep and grab the back of his collar. Next, extend your left arm in front of his face to accomplish two goals: to prevent him from moving his arm and to make him think you will grab the other side of his collar to execute a choke.

When he tries to fight off the attempted choke, Sauer says, open your legs and "climb" up his body. That will prevent him from escaping while you trap his extended arm and swing your left leg over his head. The armbar is executed when you use your hips and back to hyperextend his arm. For added security, keep your lower legs flexed to limit his chances for escape.

Role Reversal

Sauer has a preferred method for reversing the mount quickly and efficiently, and it also involves a bit of subterfuge. Start with your opponent in your guard. Sink your right hand in and grab the right side of his collar, then insert your left hand and grasp the left side. If he does not detect the danger of the choke, go ahead and execute it. He'll tap in a few seconds.

However, a savvy opponent will sense the danger and straighten his back to escape. That's your cue to let go with your left hand and begin shifting your weight onto the left side of your body. Immediately wrap your right arm around his extended right arm, thrust your hips against his chest and rotate your trunk counterclockwise. He will be swept to the mat, and you will land on top of him. From that mounted position, any number of finishing techniques can be employed.

Clean Sweep

If you are holding your opponent in the closed guard, another way to deceive him starts with planting your hands on opposite sides of his collar for a possible choke and pulling his upper body in close. If he reacts by attempting a lapel choke of his own, place your heels on his hips and straighten your legs to sweep his base out from under him. He will wind up flat on his stomach, unable to defend against your frontal choke.

Opposites Attack

Brazilian jiu-jitsu is all about options, Sauer says. If a technique is blocked, you must be ready to instantly transition into one that is just as effective. For example, you set your opponent up for an armbar by holding him in your guard and using your right hand to grab the right side of his collar and your left arm to pin his right arm against your chest. Most likely, he will climb to his feet in an attempt to pass the guard. As he uses his arms to push downward on your stomach, maintain your hold on his right arm and collar.

Next, place your left foot on your opponent's right hip, turn your body sideways and focus your attention on the opposite side of his body, Sauer says. "Wrap your right leg around his left arm and lock your legs in a triangle around it," he says.

Then grab his left leg with your right arm and, if he tries to step over your head, send him tumbling headfirst onto the mat. "He will roll and end up on his back in an armbar," Sauer says. If necessary, you can hold his left leg for extra control, he adds.

Changing Targets

Sauer's final bit of jiu-jitsu trickery also starts with you on your back and your opponent in your guard. If he inserts his left arm between your right leg and his own ribs in an attempt to pass the guard, use your right hand to grab the right side of his collar and your left hand to control his right arm. As soon as he maneuvers his left arm under your right thigh and grabs your lapel, bend your right leg around his neck and lock on a triangle choke.

If your opponent is well-schooled in Brazilian jiu-jitsu, he will probably straighten his back and try to stand. That may eliminate the pressure on his neck, but you will still have control of his right arm. To finish him, simply reverse your triangle choke so that instead of tucking your right foot behind your left knee, you now tuck your left foot behind your right knee and apply pressure to his hyperextended arm. "It's basically the same triangle hold," Sauer says. "It's just being done on the arm."

Common Mistakes

"One of the most frequent mistakes fighters make when they try to execute these five techniques is using too much power," Sauer says. "When you rely on your muscles, it's yours against his, so you will find a lot of resistance if he is stronger."

The trick is to focus on where your body is in relation to his so you can use your brain to overcome his strength, he says. "If you look for the correct body position, you have more leverage to accomplish your techniques."

If you are unfortunate enough to get caught in one of these locks during training, remember that the consequences can range from a bit of pain to a minor bruise to a dislocated joint, Sauer says. "You really can get hurt, so to stay safe, it's wise to tap before you even feel the pressure." That way, you will ensure that you're always in top condition to master the best Brazilian-jiu-jitsu deception techniques for fighting from the guard.

SURVIVAL SPORT FOR WOMEN
by Adrienne Lee Bell • Black Belt • April 2002

A 29-year-old woman was attacked while running along a beach in San Diego, when a naked 190-pound man unexpectedly jumped out from behind a bush. The assailant managed to wrestle the woman onto her back. After several seconds of struggling, she took a deep breath. Mistaking her deep breathing for a sigh of surrender, the attacker briefly lifted his head away from her body. When he did, the woman planted her fist into his face. He immediately released the iron grip he had on her waist.

Recognizing that moment as a turning point in her struggle, the woman arched her hips upward and pushed the attacker away. By maneuvering the man's body with her hip and leg strength, she was able to roll him off her and onto his back. She then sprang to her feet and fled from her worst nightmare.

The attacker did not think his victim would fight back, and that certainly worked to the woman's advantage. But she had another ace up her sleeve, one which she still credits for her quick escape: Rorion Gracie's RapeSafe program.

Jiu-Jitsu in America

Gracie is the Brazilian martial artist responsible for introducing his family's brand of *jiu-jitsu* in the United States. In 1993 he helped create the Ultimate Fighting Championship, a mixed-martial arts event designed to test the practicality and durability of his art when pitted against more traditional systems. The bouts were conceived as realistic representations of a street fight, and they did not end until one contender knocked the other out or forced him to submit.

Gracie entered his younger brother Royce, then 27, in the first few UFCs. Royce Gracie's adroit movement on the mat made him appear invincible. Tipping the scale at a meager 178 pounds, he defeated Dan Severn, a wrestler who outweighed him by 80 pounds. The victory proved to the awestruck audience that size and strength did not guarantee victory on the ground.

Royce Gracie's ground-fighting tactics rapidly garnered attention from sports fans and martial artists alike. Women in particular stood up and took notice not only of the ground techniques but also of the art's scientific upright self-defense methods.

"After the first Ultimate Fighting Championship, I just had to learn a little of that [art]," says Meg Thayer, 41, a screenwriter and martial artist from Southern California. Thayer went straight to the source: the Gracie

Jiu-Jitsu Academy in Torrance, California. There, Rorion Gracie advised her to enroll in RapeSafe, his eight-week self-defense course based on the jiu-jitsu tactics that worked so well in the UFC. Because he had recently reconfigured the family art into a methodic self-defense system specifically designed for women, Gracie said it would be an excellent way for Thayer to learn the fundamentals.

"[Because] Gracie jiu-jitsu is a sport that relies on leverage rather than strength, it is also an effective self-defense system for women of small stature," Gracie said.

Thayer enrolled in RapeSafe and the men's open jiu-jitsu class. She claims the ground fighting she learned in RapeSafe was comparable to the techniques taught in the men's course. "It is very practical for women since they have very good lower-body strength," she says.

The RapeSafe curriculum recreates 12 dangerous situations a woman might find herself in and teaches the most effective ways out. Six of those scenarios are standing, and six are horizontal, meaning the victim is lying on her back. Because of space limitations, only five of those defensive methods and techniques will be discussed in this article.

Resistance Is Not Futile

Controlling where your body goes is important in any fight. "If an attacker can pull me toward him and keep me off-balance, I am vulnerable," Thayer says.

Consequently, it is no accident that the first lesson Gracie teaches is how to create a strong base. "If a woman doesn't know how to stand properly, she makes it very easy for an attacker to drag her into a car, dark alley or building," he says. The following are his tips for attaining stability on your feet:
- Stand with your knees slightly bent.
- Angle your feet so they are perpendicular to the front of the assailant's body, and place them a little more than shoulder-width apart.
- If the attacker pushes you, lean in the direction of his force.
- As the intensity of the push increases, the intensity of your resistance must also increase.

"If you brace your legs and position your body [properly], the attacker will have one hell of a time getting you to go where he wants you to go," Gracie says.

The Slap

Once you've mastered the base, you are ready for the RapeSafe slap technique. Gracie elected to include it in his program because it's simple and it makes sense. "Unless you know how to throw a proper punch, it is safer for you to hit with an open-hand slap than with a closed fist," he says.

He reasons that the bones in your attacker's head are much harder than those in your hand. Hence, whenever your clenched fist makes contact with his hard head, especially if you throw your punch in a less-than-perfect way, it is your hand that absorbs most of the punishment. Here's how Gracie advises his students to execute the slap:

- Begin by adopting the base stance described above.
- Loosely dangle the arm you will use to slap the assailant.
- Slightly rotate your shoulders to launch the arm on its trajectory toward the target.
- Once the arm is fully extended and traveling at maximum speed, make contact with your hand. Your palm should collide with the attacker's ear, thus causing a stinging sensation on the surface and a ringing sound inside.

Be forewarned that wearing thick gloves can severely reduce the effectiveness of the slap. That's why it is seldom seen in mixed-martial arts events, in which grappling gloves are now mandated. However, Gracie teaches the slap for self-defense because women seldom walk the streets with padded gloves on their hands.

Escaping From a Front Choke

Because it is common for male attackers to choke their female victims, Gracie made certain that RapeSafe contained surefire defenses against the basic stranglehold. The one described below is intended for situations in which the assailant stands in front of you and clasps his fingers around your throat:

- Start by clenching your teeth. Tightening your jaw causes your neck muscles to contract.
- Step away from the attacker and simultaneously bend forward at the waist.
- Forcibly turn your head to the side and maneuver it out of harm's way by slipping it under the attacker's arm.

If the environment or the attacker prevents you from escaping, you can break his grip by reaching behind your neck and peeling off one of the fingers of his choking hand. Then simply bend it backward to force him to his knees, where he can be stunned with a quick knee thrust to the face.

Strangled on the Ground

For chokes that take place on the ground, RapeSafe offers a different but equally effective response. It begins with you lying on your back and

your assailant sitting on your abdomen:
- Choose either of his arms and trap it with both hands. At the same time and on the same side of his body, place your heel on the outside of his foot.
- Arch your back and thrust your hips upward, causing him to pitch forward.
- Roll on your shoulder so you eject his body in the direction of his trapped arm and leg.
- After he lands on the bottom and you rise to the top, scramble to your feet while you control his knees with your hands. Then make your escape.

A Knife on the Ground

Because women often fall or get knocked down before they are attacked with a weapon, RapeSafe teaches an efficacious knife defense for times when you're on your back and your attacker is kneeling near your feet:
- Immediately raise your hands in a defensive posture.
- As soon as the situation allows, grab the wrist of the assailant's knife hand using your closest hand.
- Sit up and wrap your other arm over his shoulder, then lock that hand onto your other wrist.
- Lie back down and rotate your upper body to leverage his knife hand behind his back.
- After inducing a sufficient amount of pain using the shoulder lock, take away his immobilized knife. You can then use it to attack him or bargain for your escape.

Mental Component

The worst part of being attacked is feeling helpless because you don't know what to do, Gracie says. Our society affords males many opportunities to learn about the options for offense and defense, but it isn't quite so fair when it comes to women.

That's why women need to enroll in a course that will provide them with a comprehensive overview of the types of dangerous situations in which they may find themselves, as well as a rundown of the best defenses for those situations. Gracie is quick to point out that once you have acquired even a basic measure of familiarity, your common sense and ability to relax under pressure will become your best tools for self-preservation.

PROVING GROUND
Rorion Gracie Updates Brazilian Jiu-jitsu Competition for 21st-Century America

by Daniel Duarte and Robert W. Young • Photos by Ivo Barata • Black Belt October 2002

Brazilian *jiu-jitsu* thrives in America because of the dreams and aspirations of one person: Rorion Gracie.

He was the first man to transport the popular grappling system from its South American homeland to the martial arts mecca of Southern California. He was the first man to take on all comers in America in style-vs.-style challenge matches designed to find out which art is most effective in real fights. He was the first man to concoct a grand plan to prove to the world that Brazilian jiu-jitsu experts are capable of defeating practitioners of any other art in no-holds-barred competition. He is the man who changed the martial arts world forever.

Brazilian Transplants

Gracie moved to America in 1978 and found that the martial arts scene was dominated by karate-style punching and kicking and, for a few eclectic practitioners, Bruce Lee's *jeet kune do*. As Gracie started teaching his father's grappling art out of his garage in Hermosa Beach, California, he was confident that one day jiu-jitsu would be an American favorite. For 10 years, he struggled to make that a reality. He drew up plans for the Gracie Jiu-Jitsu Academy, which he opened in Torrance, California, in 1989. He fought in challenge match after challenge match, always with the same result: victory.

"Because of everyone else's lack of knowledge in the ground-fighting aspect of a real fight, it was no surprise that we defeated everybody who walked

Even if the rear-naked choke does not result in a tapout, attaining the mount from the back, with both hooks placed inside the opponent's legs for three seconds, will earn the competitor four points.

through our doors," he says. "Yet there was no guarantee we would always win. Like everybody else, we were not punch-proof. One good punch could knock our fighters out, but I knew from experience that 90 percent of all fights wind up in a clinch and eventually go to the ground—which made the odds very good for [those of] us who knew Gracie jiu-jitsu."

Along the way, Gracie developed the concept of the Ultimate Fighting Championship, a multistyle tournament that would pit art against art, and in 1993 the first installment took place. He watched while younger brother Royce Gracie tapped out one opponent after another despite their background and body weight. He smiled as the rest of the martial arts community became convinced of the superiority of jiu-jitsu's ground game, which was evidenced by the art's rapid conquest of the fighting world.

"Everybody now does jiu-jitsu," he says. "They talk about passing the guard and defending the guard. They are all experts on how to attack and defend from the mount. Ground grappling has never been so popular, and that is because my father, Helio Gracie, made it very simple. I'm happy the message came through, and although some people call it by a variety of names, jiu-jitsu is the fastest-growing and most-recognized martial art in the world today."

Then Rorion Gracie watched while his original vision of a tournament in which one martial artist faced another with few technical limitations and no time limits morphed into the rule-heavy mixed-martial arts extravaganzas of today. He watched as steroid-reeking uber-athletes exploited the new ground-and-pound strategy and rose to the top. He watched as technique and finesse flew out the window.

Martial artists interested in learning from and participating in matches involving regular people, not supermen, were forced to abandon the big mixed-martial arts events in favor of traditional grappling tournaments. That is unfortunate, Gracie says, because those tournaments are guided primarily by Brazilian

To receive three points for the cross side mount, the practitioner must have control of his opponent for three seconds.

Left: The mount from the front will net the competitor four points only if he has both knees and feet on the mat for three seconds. Right: The position will be deemed incomplete if one foot is resting on the opponent's thigh.

jiu-jitsu rules, which makes them a complicated affair. Furthermore, he adds, their outcomes are frequently subjective.

Keeping the Focus

The International Gracie Jiu-Jitsu Federation was founded with the purpose of organizing competitive events that will help its members, associates and supporters understand and pursue excellence in combat. The first IGJJF Open Championship, scheduled to take place in February 2003 in Los Angeles, will operate under a set of rules designed to bring the focus back to the original concept of the Gracie family: Competitions should reward technique, and competitors should pursue the submission.

The Open Championship will give mixed-martial arts fans a chance to witness the technical side of ground fighting,

As long as one leg is trapped between his opponent's legs, the competitor on top will not receive points for attaining the cross side mount.

a facet of combat that is not always displayed in no-holds-barred shows in which art takes a back seat to brute strength. "Often, we see a fight degenerate to the ground-and-pound," Gracie says. "No technique [is used] to finish the opponent, and that is what a lot of fans are missing."

He also sees the IGJJF's new tournaments as a vehicle for everyday jiu-jitsu practitioners around the world to keep polishing their skills and not lose focus of what the art is all about. "Some people want to get in shape or lose weight, some people like the competition aspect of it, [while others] like the philosophy of the art—but it's all irrelevant," he says. "The reason the Gracies have been teaching jiu-jitsu for the past 80 years is to get the average person better prepared to defend himself in a real fight."

Unfortunately, that simple concept seems to have fallen by the wayside in a large part of the Brazilian-jiu-jitsu world. "In today's tournaments, for example, a person scores a couple points or even an advantage, and if he holds onto that for the remainder of the round, he becomes the winner," Gracie says. "He is the new world champion, but in some cases, he knows deep down that if the fight had lasted another 30 seconds, he could have lost. That is not a convincing victory."

Wearing the title of world champion should leave no doubt about who is the world's best, but that does not always happen these days, Gracie says. The IGJJF aims to remedy that.

The organization will also attempt to do away with interference and distraction. At regular Brazilian jiu-jitsu tournaments, it's not uncommon to see coaches or trainers on the sidelines screaming at the referees to award a point or advantage to their competitor. And they often succumb to the pressure. Under the new rules of the IGJJF, that won't happen. Either the competitor scores a clear point with the right positioning or the point is

Rorion Gracie's new rules of competition dictate that one person may not hold his opponent's sleeves with the intent of stalling.

not awarded because the position was not 100 percent. Nothing is open to interpretation or coercion.

New Rules for an Old Game

To fix those nagging problems, Gracie devised a set of rules to govern the game:
- There are no time limits or advantage points.
- The cross side mount receives three points. The competitor must have control of his opponent for three seconds.
- The mount from the front receives four points. The competitor must have both knees and feet on the ground for three seconds.
- The mount from the back receives four points. The competitor must have both knees and feet on the ground, or he must have both hooks placed inside the opponent's legs for three seconds.
- The competitor may not hold both of the opponent's sleeves at any time with the intent of stalling. The referee reserves the right to give two warnings for stalling, which will count as two faults. The competitor then has five seconds to release the sleeves. The third warning will lead to disqualification.
- The competitor inside the opponent's guard must try to pass the guard, and the competitor on the bottom must attack. If after five minutes the competitor on top cannot pass the guard, the referee will reverse the position. If at the five-minute mark the top competitor is at the half-guard position, the fight will not be interrupted. However, if he is placed back in the guard, the position will be reversed.
- If a competitor is on top of a cross-mount position and cannot accomplish the mount or stops attacking for more than 60 seconds, the match will be interrupted and he will have to choose one of two options: to pass or to defend the guard.
- If a competitor is in the top-mount position and cannot effect a submission and if he stops attacking for more than 60 seconds, the match will be interrupted and he will have to choose one of three options: to assume the top cross-mount position, to pass the guard or to defend the guard.
- Foot locks are permitted. Knee locks are permitted for brown and black belts. Ankle locks are not allowed.
- Immediate disqualification will result from deliberate bending of the fingers or toes, hair pulling, striking, biting, pressure-point attacks, eye gouges and groin shots.
- Immediate disqualification will also result from disrespectful gestures or verbal abuse directed at a referee, competitor or spectator.

- Matches will end with a tapout, when 12 points are accumulated or by referee intervention (disqualification).

Opportunity of a Lifetime

Gracie is certain that the new tournament format will attract the top jiu-jitsu competitors in the world. Three of them have already committed to show: 20-year-old Ryron Gracie, 18-year-old Rener Gracie and 16-year-old Ralek Gracie. The sons of Rorion Gracie are well on their way to becoming the next generation of Brazilian-jiu-jitsu champs.

All winners of the Open Championship will receive cash prizes and medals, but up to nine of them will be treated to a special reward: a weeklong all-expenses-paid trip to Brazil to train at Helio Gracie's ranch. "I think all people who are enthusiasts of jiu-jitsu worldwide will look forward to the opportunity to study with the originator of the art," Rorion Gracie says. "It's going to be like staying at Michael Jordan's house for a week of training in basketball."

ARE YOU A NON-GRACIE GRAPPLER?

The IGJJF Open Championship is just that: open. Anyone who studies Brazilian *jiu-jitsu*, judo, submission grappling, shootwrestling or any other ground-based art is eligible to enter as long as the rules are obeyed. All belt ranks and experience levels are welcome. All competitors must wear a white or blue uniform.

Although some practitioners might think they won't fit in with the Gracie clan because they happen to train under a second- or third-generation Brazilian or American, there's no need to worry, Rorion Gracie says. "Don't turn down an invitation for a party at the Playboy Mansion because you think all the girls are too cute for you. Go to the party anyway!"

—D.D.

GRACIES IN ACTION
Up-to-the-Minute Updates on the First Family of the Mixed Martial Arts
by Jake Rossen • Black Belt • September 2004

Mention ultimate fighting or the martial arts in general, and the first thing that pops into the layperson's head will probably be a *gi*-clad Royce Gracie twisting bodybuilders into pretzels. That iconic image—a product of brother Rorion Gracie's original Ultimate Fighting Championship arena—ushered in a new era for self-defense. Sure, everyone had heard of obscure maneuvers that could down even the roughest brawler, but until then, live demonstrations had never been televised to a quarter-million homes on pay-per-view.

A decade later, the Gracies' core art of Brazilian *jiu-jitsu* remains a necessity for anyone thinking of stepping into a freestyle fighting arena. Every martial athlete considers it as integral to his training as running, eating and sleeping. Find yourself in the octagon without knowledge of how to apply and defend against a triangle choke or armbar, and you'll likely find yourself taking home the loser's purse.

Although the family members who helped shape jiu-jitsu for a new generation have little left to prove, the Gracies aren't content to pass their time recalling their glory days. They're as busy as ever, and *Black Belt* raced to catch up.

Rickson

Long thought of as the undisputed family champion, Rickson Gracie has cultivated an image of invincibility. The best submission grapplers in the world have walked away humbled after training sessions, and many have proclaimed him to have no equal on the ground. Being held in such regard doesn't seem to be sufficient motivation to compete onstage, however, for Rickson has not fought since a successful clash with Pancrase legend Masakatsu Funaki in 2000.

Although the offers have poured in, especially concerning a matchup with "Gracie Hunter" Kazushi Sakuraba, Rickson has chosen to keep a low profile. Many speculate that, at age 45, he has little left to achieve in the ring. As of late, he's has been taking on a far more visible role in his Los Angeles academy, teaching two or three times per week. This may be in response to K-1's having offered a substantial purse for his retirement fight. After appearing in that organization's event to address the audience earlier in the year, he may treat us to one last chance to see his unique expression of jiu-jitsu. (www.rickson.com)

Royce

While brother Rickson receives the lion's share of accolades in Japan, the United States regards Royce Gracie as not only the most recognizable Gracie but also perhaps the most respected martial artist since Bruce Lee. In a sensational display of attrition, he stepped into Japan's PRIDE ring on New Year's Eve 2003 to avenge a controversial loss to judo gold-medalist Hidehiko Yoshida. To the amazement of the crowd, Royce stripped off his gi top for the first time in competition. It would not be Royce's kryptonite, as some speculated, but Yoshida's. Battering him from corner to corner, Royce earned a recorded draw and an unrecorded victory—and capped 10 years of mixed-martial arts stardom.

That fight interrupted Royce's day job, which is traveling the globe to conduct seminars. This year, he'll see the United Kingdom, Italy, Israel, Spain, Japan and plenty of cities in the States. When he's not busy educating civilians, he tackles weeklong law-enforcement seminars. All that business won't prevent him from accepting an offer from PRIDE or K-1, however, and he's keeping his schedule open to fight again late in the year. (www.roycegracie.tv)

Royler

Ending a three-year drought from MMA competition, Royler Gracie stepped into the ring on three weeks' notice in May 2004 to face the highly lauded Genki Sudo. The marquee bout took place in K-1's inaugural MMA

Royler Gracie

show. Unfortunately, the level of competition in the sport makes it difficult to return after such a long layoff. Sudo stuffed Royler's numerous takedown attempts before landing a knee and a succession of strikes that prompted Royler's first KO loss in the ring.

Already back and traveling for seminars, Royler remains optimistic about his future in MMA and plans to head back to Brazil to think things through. "I liked the fight but not the result," he says, with a laugh. "If I want to fight again, I need to stop teaching, lift weights a little more. I'd like a rematch, but maybe get one fight in before that. Then I'll train for Genki. I'll put his picture in my wallet." (www.roylergracie.com)

Rorion

Having co-created the UFC back in 1993 and used that platform to launch Brazilian jiu-jitsu into the mainstream, Rorion Gracie will never lack for business interests. Still running the original Gracie Jiu-Jitsu Academy in Torrance, California, he recently opened the Gracie Museum in the same location to display valued pieces of his family's history. August 28 and 29, 2004, will see the return of the Gracie Jiu-Jitsu Tournament in Lynwood, California, with rules encouraging a high level of activity. On September 10-12, 2004, Rorion will host a Gracie cruise that will offer instruction from himself and his father, Helio, on the open seas.

Back at home, sons Ryron (22), Rener (20) and Ralek (18) are combining an instinctual grasp of the grappling art with strapping frames. "They keep busy teaching classes and seminars, and they are all eagerly waiting for their debut in the no-holds-barred arena," Rorion says. "They have been training with and without their gi in the newly built octagon we have at the academy."

Ralph

Dubbed "The Pitbull" in honor of the time he had to subdue an angry canine, Ralph Gracie made his return to MMA in late 2003 after a seven-year hiatus. He nabbed a lauded decision victory over top-10-ranked Dokonjonosuke Mishima in a seesaw fight that helped launch PRIDE's sister show, Bushido. Pundits who scoffed at Ralph's chances after such a long layoff were silenced … for a bit.

In May 2004 Ralph confronted top lightweight Takanori Gomi. In keeping with his aggressive style, he went after Gomi at the opening bell but was met with a series of knees that put him down and out instantly. That flurry may have ended the fight, but it also ended the debate over whether the Gracies are reluctant to face top competition. Back in California, Ralph has cultivated a franchise of successful schools, with academies in San Francisco, Dublin, Mountain View and Antioch. Said to be training harder than ever, he looks forward to more fights in Japan. (www.ralphgracie.com)

Renzo

Stop by Renzo Gracie's school in midtown Manhattan, and you'll be amazed at how affable a room full of dangerous submission artists can be. And why not? Renzo himself is as gregarious and cordial as ever, even though a knee injury has sidelined his fight career for the moment. He last stepped into the ring in October 2003, when he lost a decision to Carlos Newton that some think he should have won. These days, he trains brothers Ryan and Ralph for their busy schedules and looks for an opportunity to get back in the action. Students Matt Serra and Ricardo Almeida continue to make waves in MMA arenas. (www.renzogracie.com)

Rodrigo

Leading the charge of the next generation of Gracies to step into MMA, Rodrigo Gracie complements his jiu-jitsu with excellent stand-up and positional skills. His perfect 4-0 record in PRIDE is even more impressive considering it includes dangerous submission artist Daiju Takase and the accomplished Hayato Sakurai. Rodrigo's success caught the eye of rival Japanese promotion K-1, which recently signed him to a deal. Watch for his debut there sometime in the fall. (www.rodrigogracie.com)

Ryan

Look up "intensity" in the dictionary, and you're likely to find a picture of Ryan Gracie providing a helpful visual. He's constantly in demand in Japan, battling a laundry list of the nation's hometown heroes. Most recently, he won a controversial split decision against Ikuhisa Minowa in PRIDE's Bushido show.

Preparing for a fight usually means meeting up with brother Renzo at the latter's Manhattan academy. Otherwise, Ryan attends to his own school in Sao Paulo, Brazil. Expect him to continue his rivalry with Japan's best in upcoming events.

Cesar

If the name doesn't sound familiar, it may be because Cesar Gracie hasn't yet stepped into the MMA arena as a competitor. Don't be fooled, though: He just might be the most influential Gracie of the new millennium. His academy in Pleasant Hill, California, has produced some of the best up-and-comers in recent memory. Nick Diaz made his UFC debut in April by knocking out hammerfisted Robbie Lawler. Even Diaz supporters thought he'd win by submission, but such is the all-angles training Cesar gives his students.

Fellow Team Cesar standout David Terrell is set to square off against top-ranked middleweight Matt Lindland in an August 2004 UFC. And if Cesar winds up never stepping on the mat, it won't be for lack of trying. He continues to pursue a bout with Frank Shamrock that would give promoters that valuable "Gracie vs. Shamrock" marquee made famous by Royce and Ken in the mid-1990s. If Cesar has his way, history will definitely repeat itself. (www.graciefighter.com)

THE HOUSE THAT GRACIE BUILT
Rorion and Royce Gracie During the Early Years of the Ultimate Fighting Championship
by Don Duarte • Black Belt • August 2006

"This is my house. I built it!"
—Royce Gracie, in a current UFC commercial

"A lot of new UFC fans don't even know who Royce Gracie is."
—Joe Rogan, UFC commentator

Even though the popularity of the Ultimate Fighting Championship is at an all-time high, a large portion of the Spike TV generation of fans doesn't know who Royce Gracie is or how he contributed to the creation of the event and the sport of mixed martial arts. But to the old hands, Royce is the martial artist who put the UFC on the map, the first champion to emerge from the gladiator days before the implementation of time limits, weight classes and rules. When only one fighter was left standing at the end of an eight- or 16-man tournament, he ruled supreme. Those early days saw him win three out of the first four tournaments with a style that was so different it was a shock to the system.

"I thought I knew martial arts until I saw the UFC," says Joe Rogan, UFC commentator and host of TV's *Fear Factor*. "But after I saw Royce Gracie fight, I realized that I knew nothing."

Before the UFC, American audiences' only exposure to the martial arts was the flashy punching and kicking featured in fight flicks. The *Kung Fu* TV series helped solidify striking with the hands and feet as the staple of the martial arts, as well as enshroud those skills in mystery and mysticism. That conception was furthered when the supernatural acrobatics of Hong Kong's Kung Fu Theatre reached American shores.

But if Royce built the house of UFC, then his older brother, Rorion Gracie, was the architect who surveyed the land and drew up the plans for it. Long before Dana White and the Fertitta brothers came on the scene, the style-vs.-style showdown was the lofty ambition of a skinny Brazilian kid who dreamed of putting his father's martial art on a world stage.

Rorion's Trek

In 1969, 17-year-old Rorion, eldest son of Helio Gracie, visited California for a three-month vacation. When his money and return ticket were stolen, he found himself doing odd jobs, from flipping hamburgers to construction.

The trip stretched to a year and was packed with experiences, including panhandling and sleeping on street corners.

Eventually, Rorion flew back to Rio de Janeiro, Brazil, to complete his studies. After graduating from law school in 1978, he opted to return to America. This time, however, his mind was set on educating the masses about the benefits of his family's fighting art. He realized that accomplishing that mission would entail grabbing the public's attention, and in the States, that's never easy to do.

After his first few months back in California, Rorion got a break and started working as an extra in movies and TV shows, including *Hart to Hart*, *Fantasy Island*, *Three's Company* and *Lethal Weapon*. For the next 10 years, he was a frequent face on the back lots of Warner Bros. and Universal Studios.

He also set up some mats in his garage.

Jiu-Jitsu Arrives

Word of a guy from Brazil teaching a unique martial art in a garage in Hermosa Beach, California, quickly spread. He always presented his moves with a smile, but Rorion's effectiveness was no joke. He was so confident in his teachings that he offered a free introductory class to everyone he met. Sure that each new student would be hooked, he ended the classes by saying, "Bring a friend and get another free class, or 10 friends and 10 free classes." His arguments about the importance of ground fighting, backed up by his leave-no-doubt demonstrations, were almost always enough to convince people to give it a try. When talking to hard-core martial arts traditionalists, he would often sweeten the deal by including an invitation to sample some fresh watermelon juice at his home after class.

People from every martial arts background soon began flocking to Rorion's "garage academy." On many occasions, when excited students would share their experiences with friends, their former instructors would push for the opportunity to unmask the slender Brazilian. Rorion wound up inviting many a pupil to watch a match in which he would effortlessly submit the challenger—as humanely as possible.

The Art Expands

Rorion wrote and produced a two-volume documentary titled *Gracie Jiu-Jitsu in Action*, which presented footage of real fights in which he and his brothers arm-locked or choked out everyone in their path. With a small advertisement placed in a martial arts magazine, they reached practitioners around the world. The buzz had gone international.

By 1985, the number of students had risen so much that Rorion needed to recruit Royce, then 17, to help out. By the summer of 1989, half-hour private lessons were being scheduled Monday through Sunday from 7 a.m. to 9 p.m. More than 150 students were visiting the garage regularly, and another 100 were on a waiting list. Among them was writer/director John Milius (*Conan the Barbarian, Apocalypse Now, Red Dawn*), who would later become involved with the UFC production. Rorion knew it was time to bring brothers Rickson and Royler on board to help him establish the official Gracie Jiu-jitsu Academy in Torrance, California. Meanwhile, keeping with the family tradition, Rorion had already sired seven children.

One day, Rorion realized that he'd arrived at a pivotal point in his crusade: Should he make his family's techniques available on video, thus revealing what were essentially trade secrets, or should he keep them for his family and students so potential opponents wouldn't have access to the intricacies of the system? The latter option, he knew, most likely would keep the Gracies winning for years to come.

Rorion concluded that his family's grappling art was too beneficial not to be shared. If people chose to learn the system so they could one day use it against the Gracies, that would reflect positively on the family's proficiency as teachers, he figured.

Ultimate Fighting Championship

In 1993, after 15 years of laying the groundwork to put Gracie jiu-jitsu on the map in America, Rorion created the Ultimate Fighting Championship. Not long afterward, *Forbes* magazine declared it the most successful franchise in pay-per-view history.

But merely launching the event wasn't enough for Rorion. He wanted to drive home his point that Gracie jiu-jitsu was so effective and efficient it could enable even an average-size 170-pounder to take on bigger and stronger opponents. With Royce's success in the first four UFCs, Rorion knew he'd accomplished his mission. He'd captured America's attention and proved that Gracie jiu-jitsu was the best fighting method in the world.

Royce's UFC success spawned widespread interest in Gracie jiu-jitsu. While many students traveled to Torrance to train at the academy and the brothers crisscrossed the country to conduct seminars, jiu-jitsu schools sprang up everywhere. The growing popularity of the art and grappling tournaments finally signaled to the mainstream that Gracie jiu-jitsu ruled the roost. It left a plethora of traditional schools scrambling to incorporate the basics of jiu-jitsu into their curricula.

The soaring popularity also caught the attention of military spec-ops units and law-enforcement agencies. The U.S. Army and several police academies ended up adopting Gracie jiu-jitsu as their official combatives program. Rorion's GARD course—standing for Gracie Air Rage Defense—was being used to teach pilots and flight attendants how to control unruly passengers long before September 11, 2001. His Women Empowered course became popular among women worried about sexual assault.

Evolution of the Revolution

While Rorion watched his father's jiu-jitsu grow in popularity, first in America and then worldwide, the ground began to rumble beneath the UFC's foundation in a manner that made it veer from the path Rorion had envisioned.

Beginning with the UFC 5, then co-owner Semaphore Entertainment Group insisted on time limits for the bouts. Although the longest fight had been just more than 15 minutes (for the championship of the UFC 4), the new 30-minute limit directly precipitated the longest bout in UFC history: The stronger and heavier Ken Shamrock held down Royce for 30 minutes in what some deemed a transparent effort to win bragging rights of having gone the distance with the champ.

Seeing the writing on the wall, Rorion made a quick exit from the UFC.

"My father had started the first Federation of Jiu-Jitsu back in Brazil to promote sportive competition," Rorion says. "But then he stepped down from his post as its first president when he saw [it] moving away from his original intent, which is reality-based self-defense. I did the same with the UFC.

"You can discover a lot about a man's character when you leave him in the middle of the jungle without an expectation of rescue. Some people get busy using all their resources to survive. Others may panic and have a heart attack. But if you leave that same man in the jungle and tell him, 'I'll be back to pick you up tomorrow,' his mind-set is different. The uncertainty element is gone, and he's going to try to conserve his energy and just survive until he's rescued the next day. That's what the clock does in MMA. It tells a fighter who's losing to try to stall until the bell rings rather than use his resources to find a way to defeat his opponent."

Rorion's departure from the UFC was followed by even more changes: judges' score cards, five-minute rounds, limitations on techniques, and the elimination of the tournament format that ultimately proved which style was most effective against different opponents.

"If there had been judges' score cards and a 15-minute time limit in the UFC 4, Dan Severn would have been declared the champion for being on top of Royce for 15 minutes," Rorion says. "But as we saw, just a few seconds later, Royce got him to submit with the triangle choke."

Returning to the UFC

"By the time of Royce's last fight, he was the most prolific and influential fighter in the UFC," Rorion says. "People studied his fights and sought out Gracie jiu-jitsu training on their own. I got a lot of requests from fighters beaten by Royce to train them. Look at Kimo [Leopoldo], for example. As soon as he lost to Royce, he began learning jiu-jitsu and even bills himself today as a jiu-jitsu fighter.

"I received calls from several UFC fighters telling me they learned to ground-fight by studying my instructional tapes. So I feel satisfied in having achieved my goal of proving Gracie jiu-jitsu to be the most effective fighting style in the world. In a sense, I feel like I made it possible for the blind to see."

Future of Gracie Jiu-Jitsu

On May 27, 2006, the UFC 60 will witness Royce's return to the octagon. He'll be stripped of his *gi* and saddled with rules that weren't there when he left. He'll face Matt Hughes, a younger and more athletically gifted fighter with jiu-jitsu training of his own. It'll be interesting to see how Royce fairs against the new breed of combat athletes, especially because few pundits are giving the Brazilian much of a chance.

Meanwhile, Rorion's eldest sons continue to field offers to compete in MMA around the world, but their father doesn't believe in pressuring them. Instead, he encourages them to proceed at their own pace.

Rogan says the biggest threat to jiu-jitsu fighters like Rorion's sons is Chuck Liddell: "He's a big, strong light-heavyweight with a huge reach and knockout power. He's also difficult to take down and almost impossible to keep down."

Asked whether he's interested in facing off against the likes of Liddell, Ryron Gracie, Rorion's oldest son, says: "I think he'd make a good opponent, and I'd like a shot at him. I think it would be fun."

Grapplers like Randy Couture, who lost two out of his three encounters with Liddell, made the mistake of trying to fight Liddell's game, Rorion says. "We never try to box with a boxer. Randy was not able to properly close the distance and stay close. And while it's possible for Liddell to knock out even the best jiu-jitsu fighter—anyone can be knocked out if hit on the right spot—nine out of 10 times, a well-trained Gracie jiu-jitsu fighter will beat a striker, even one as skilled and dangerous as Chuck Liddell."

How can he be so sure? "Well, like I've been saying for the past 30 years, there is only one way to find out," Rorion says. "The proof will be in the pudding."

GRACIE UPDATE
Latest News From the Birthplace of Brazilian Jiu-Jitsu in America

Interview by Edward Pollard • Photos by Rick Hustead • Black Belt • December 2006

*I*t's been 20 years since the Gracie name started making waves in the American martial arts community and 13 since Royce Gracie first demonstrated the art at the Ultimate Fighting Championship. After a string of wins, the disappointments began as several family members fell to cross-training opponents. It seemed like years passed with nary a peep from the Gracies—until Royce entered the octagon to face Matt Hughes. And we all know how that ended.

Yet on Rorion Gracie's side of the family, business is better than ever. With the blessing of his father, Helio Gracie, Rorion and his sons have continued to run the jiu-jitsu academy that's stood on Carson Street in Torrance, California, for the past 16 years. They've refined what they're offering the public, and they've brainstormed a bunch of new products Black Belt readers are sure to be interested in. The update follows.

—*Editor*

Black Belt: What's the big news in the Gracie empire?

Rorion Gracie: We're getting ready to move the academy to a new location after 16 years. Our Internet business has grown a lot, so we need a storage and shipping area that can accommodate the demand.

BB: Where will the new academy be located?

Rorion: Five minutes north of where we are now—literally 30 seconds off the 405 freeway. It's much more accessible for everyone. It's going to be the most amazing martial arts school of all time. Our Web site will remain the same—www.gracie.com. I had to say that. (laughs)

BB: Are there any new features on your Web site?

Ralek Gracie: We just came out with a monthly newsletter, *Gracie Insider*. We're trying to keep people up to date with snippets of my brothers and me around the academy and information on techniques that we discovered and want to show people.

BB: Do you have any new DVDs in the works?

Rorion: We're releasing instructional DVDs that are revised versions of the videotapes that I did with Royce years ago.

BB: What are the differences between the originals and the revamped versions?

BLACK BELT

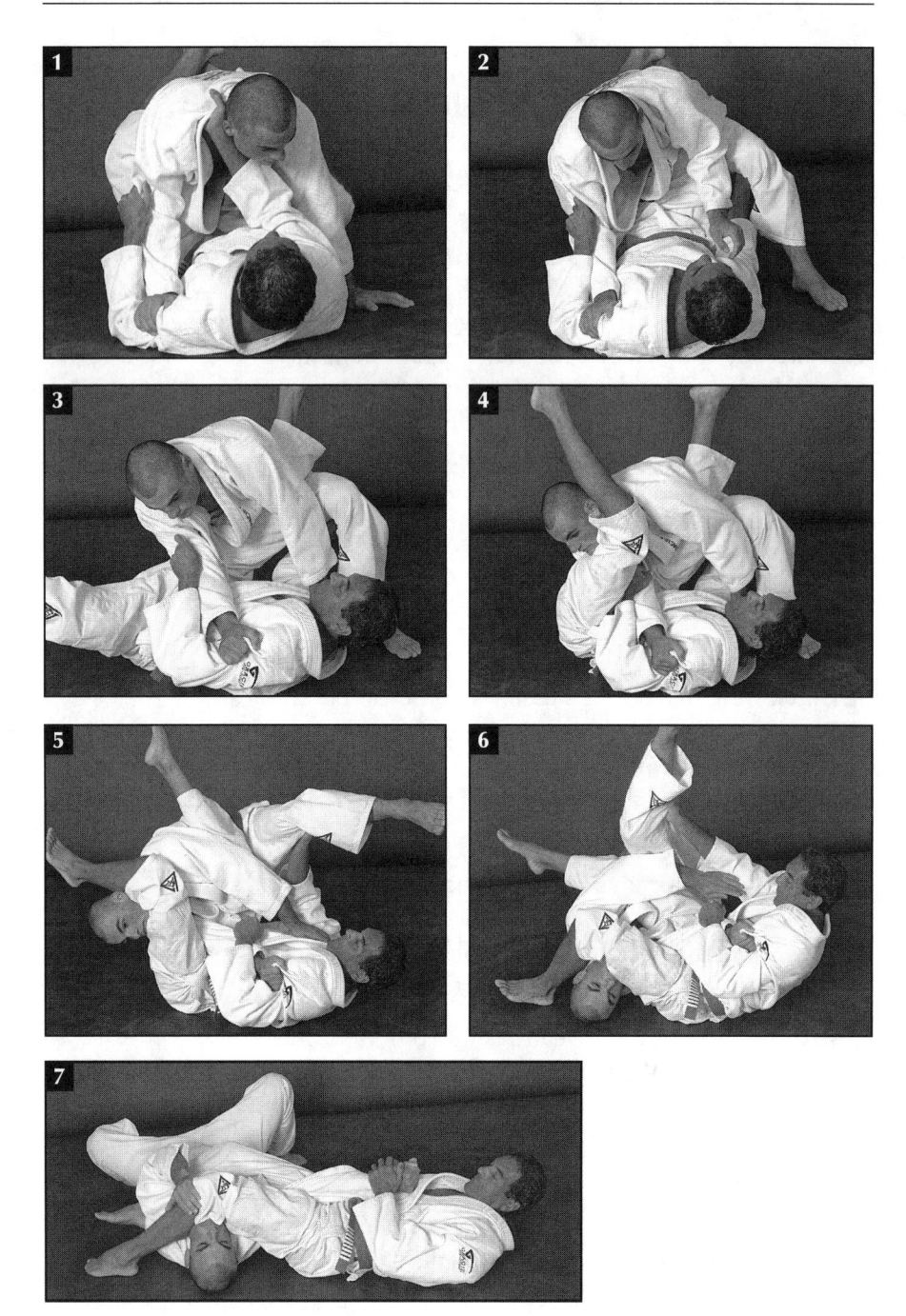

Sweep to Spinning Arm Lock: Holding Ralek Gracie in his closed guard, Rorion Gracie grabs his son's right lapel and right sleeve (1). Ralek posts his left leg to pass the guard, and Rorion underhooks it (2). Rorion then opens his guard and spins to his right (3), after which he positions his left leg over Ralek's neck (4). Next, he lifts Ralek's leg while pushing down with his own legs, causing the opponent to topple (5). Rorion follows him into a sitting position (6), then grabs his wrist and leans backward for the armbar (7).

Rorion: The content of the DVDs is the same as the old instructional tapes, but they have special, never-seen bonus footage of my sons Ryron and Rener giving tips on grappling and *jiu-jitsu* techniques. They're amazing techniques, very well presented. There are [pointers on] what your state of mind should be when you're training.

We also have a guided tour of the Gracie Museum, which is a special bonus feature for people around the world who've never had a chance to visit it. I present the tour and talk about the history of the Gracie family.

BB: Is there anything more you'd care to say about the DVDs?

Rorion: There are four different sets to the Gracie DVD collection: the basics, the intermediate [course], the advanced [course] and street self-defense. People who buy the complete collection will get 50-year-old archival footage of my father and my Uncle Carlos, a movie I thought was destroyed. I took it to a lab in Hollywood, and they were able to recover this stuff from the ashes.

And before I forget, we now have *Gracie Jiu-jitsu in Action, Volume 1* and *Volume 2* available on UMD for the Sony PlayStation Portable.

BB: Is there a Gracie video game?

Rorion: Not yet. It's all part of the project. First things first.

BB: Have you designed any new apparel?

Rorion: My sons have designed a line of clothing. They've come up with a very interesting concept called the Submission Series, which is the seven most common submission techniques used in Gracie jiu-jitsu. Each design features not only the move but also an explanation of what it's called, the consequences if it's applied on someone, and a philosophical and practical breakdown of the move—all of which is printed on a shirt.

BB: So someone standing behind you in line at the movie theater ...

Rorion: ... Is reading about the arm lock, yes.

BB: It sounds like a clever way to use what is typically treated as ad space.

Rorion: They're very popular T-shirts. We have four of the seven available. These guys are always coming up with new looks for shirts and stuff like that. We have a variety of clothing for different occasions—such as fight shorts that you can grapple or surf or swim in.

Ralek: You'll be seeing us wearing the fight shorts soon in the octagon.

BB: Ralek, are you going to fight soon?

Ralek: We're constantly training—it's just a matter of everything coming together and finding the right time. Of course, my brothers and I are getting more involved in the business—teaching, designing clothing and, for Rener, running the Web site—but we also have to train to stay on top of the game. More than anything, our goal is eventually to go in there and challenge the current people. Before that, we have a lot of missions to make happen.

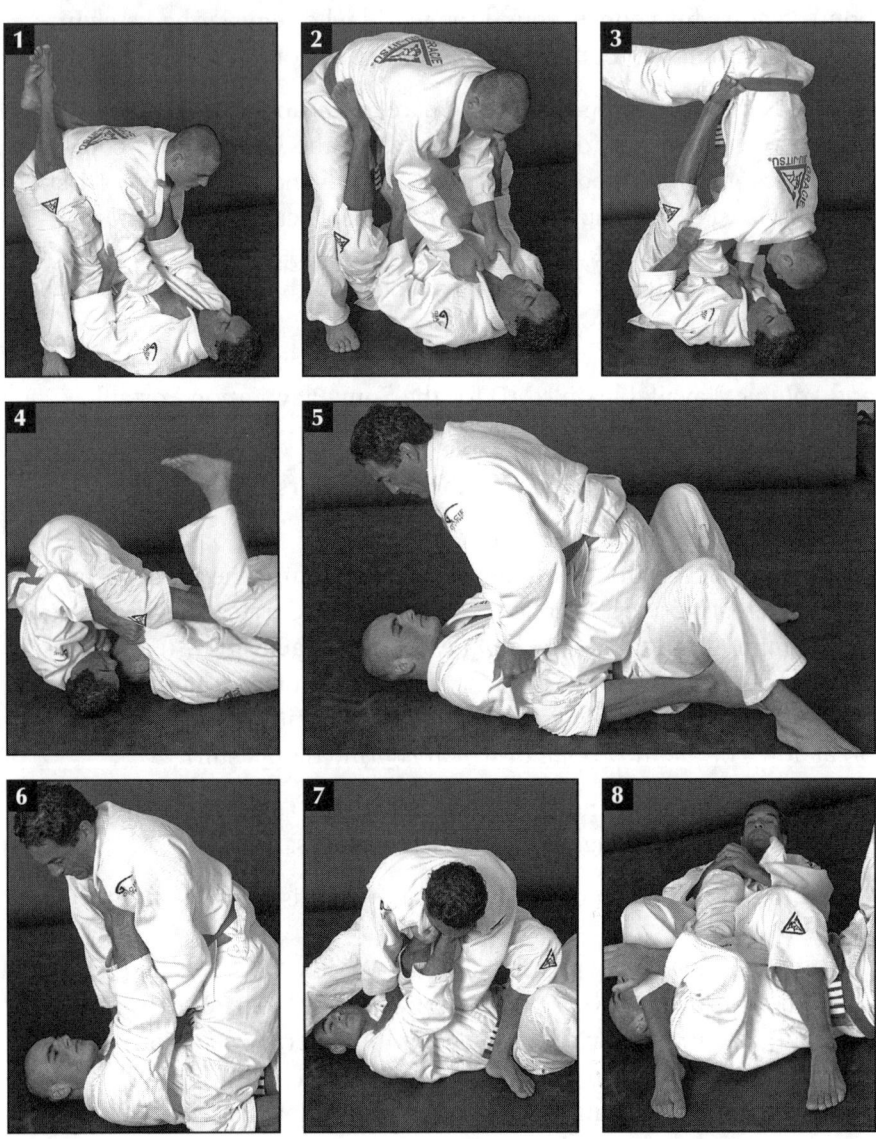

Overhead Sweep to Arm Lock: Ralek Gracie stands in Rorion Gracie's guard (1). Rorion uncrosses his ankles, drops his hips to the ground and places his feet on his opponent's hips (2). Rorion lifts with his legs (3), then drops Ralek over his right shoulder (4). Next, Rorion rolls into the full mount (5). As soon as Ralek reaches up to push Rorion off (6), Rorion places his hands on his opponent's chest and swings his right leg over his head (7) before executing the armbar (8).

THE ULTIMATE GUIDE TO BRAZILIAN JIU-JITSU

BB: Your family has obviously experienced plenty of success in mixed martial arts. It seems as though there's nothing left to prove.

Ralek: It's just a matter of competing for ourselves. I enjoy fighting; it's something I wake up thinking about. Aside from that, it's about accomplishing more for the overall movement of Gracie jiu-jitsu.

Rorion: The essence of this movement is to educate as many people as possible about the benefits of knowing Gracie jiu-jitsu. It's something that gives a person a lot of tranquility and confidence, and that can affect life in a whole bunch of ways, much more than knowing how to fight. It makes

Sit-up Sweep From the Guard: Rorion Gracie starts with Ralek Gracie in his guard (1). Rorion sits up and turns to his left, bringing his right arm over his opponent's right arm and resting his weight on his left elbow (2). He then posts on his left hand while controlling Ralek's elbow (3). He pushes off his right foot and thrusts his hips up and into the opponent's body (4). As Ralek falls onto his back, Rorion follows him (5) and establishes the full mount (6).

153

an attorney a better attorney, a doctor a better doctor, an engineer a better engineer—all because they acquire confidence from Gracie jiu-jitsu.

BB: Confidence and self-esteem are important foundations in everyone's life.

Rorion: They did so much for my dad at 140 pounds back in Brazil

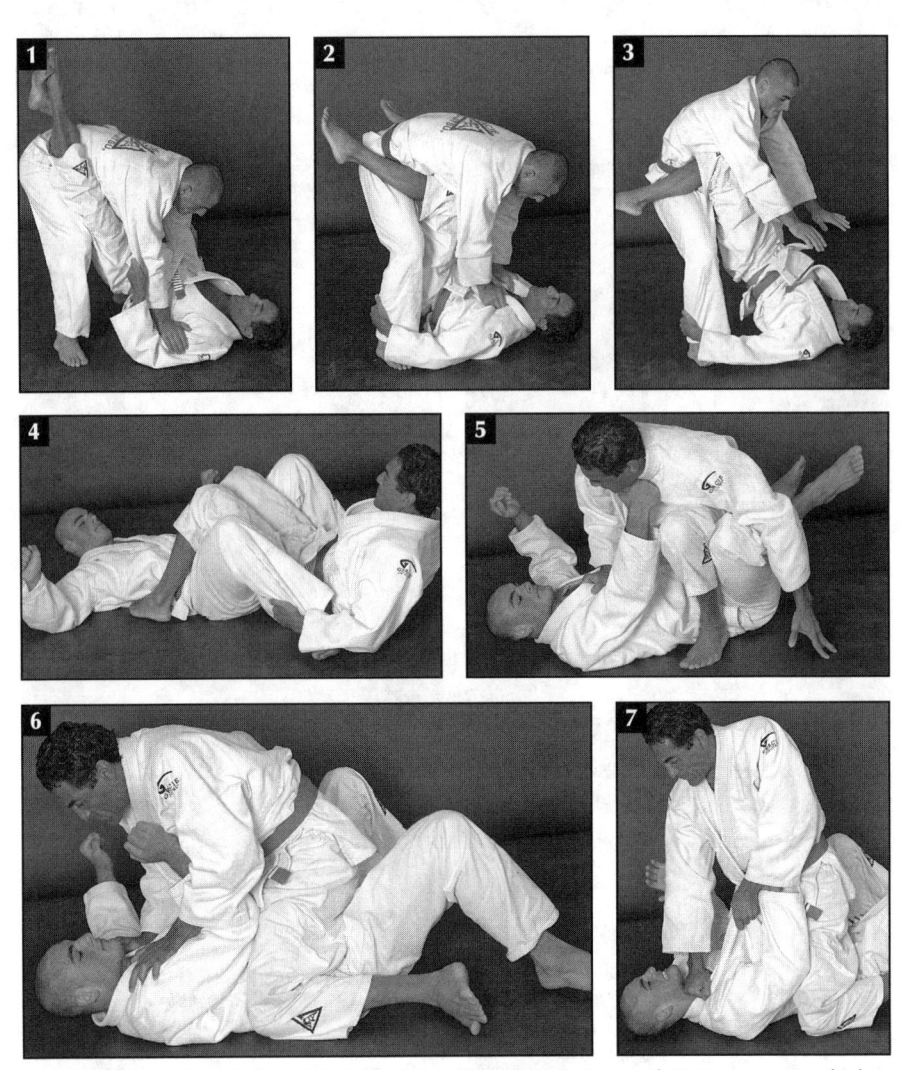

Double-Ankle Sweep From the Guard: Ralek Gracie is held in Rorion Gracie's guard (1). Rorion uncrosses his legs, places his knees against Ralek's stomach and grabs his ankles (2). Rorion then raises his hips and thrusts his knees into his opponent's stomach (3). Ralek falls backward (4), and Rorion pulls himself on top (5) to establish the full mount (6). To execute the finishing choke, Rorion grabs the opponent's left lapel with his right hand and pushes it across his throat while pulling the right lapel with his left hand (7).

that he embraced the Gracie cause of making that available for as many people as possible. That's what brought me to America, and these boys are carrying on the mission of making sure that the techniques and teachings are accessible to as many people as possible all over the world. That's the plan.

BB: What else have you been doing to further your goal of spreading jiu-jitsu?

Rorion: In October 2003, the U.S. Army officially adopted Gracie jiu-jitsu for its combatives program. Now they're unfolding it on a larger scale. It's officially part of [the training at] Fort Benning [Georgia]. We're continually traveling and certifying military instructors so they can pass the information on to other soldiers. It's been very successful because the Army is not only about shooting. Sometimes they have to shoot, sometimes they have to separate [members of opposing political or religious groups] and sometimes they have to give humanitarian aid. They just can't go in with guns and start shooting people. When they need an intermediate solution, Gracie jiu-jitsu allows them to control the situation without having to kill anyone.

BB: Training for up-close situations is important in law enforcement, too.

Rorion: That's why our program is so popular within the law-enforcement community. Everybody from the Secret Service and FBI to the DEA and Homeland Security—all regularly send their [agents] to our school.

BB: Most martial artists would have trouble handling all those projects.

Rorion: They keep us quite busy. We're also getting materials ready for the next book. We're doing a photographic essay of the Gracie family's history—newspaper clippings and photos and stuff like that. And we're co-producing a documentary on these boys.

BB: Have any new celebrities started training at the Gracie Jiu-Jitsu Academy?

Rorion: Dr. Robert Rey from *Dr. 90210* has decided to return to his roots—he's Brazilian—and take jiu-jitsu. He's doing very well. Ed O'Neill from *Married With Children* continues to choke us out regularly. People like Nicolas Cage, Michael Clarke Duncan and Shaquille O'Neal have experienced jiu-jitsu and understand what the mechanics are. They're strong supporters of the whole thing.

BB: How do you train a guy the size of Shaq?

Ralek: Just feed him the basics—that's all he needs. His strength and size carry him the rest of the way.

THE MAN WHO CHANGED THE WORLD
15 Years After the UFC Was Conceived, Royce Gracie Looks Back at How His Fighting Art Rocked the Martial Arts!

by Robert W. Young • Photos by Rick Hustead • Black Belt • January 2008

Where were you 15 years ago? According to the most recent Black Belt reader survey, many of you weren't into the martial arts yet. Some of you weren't even born. If you fall into either category, it means that everything you know about the arts has been shaped to some extent by the accomplishments of a single man: Royce Gracie.

Let's journey back to the pre-Royce era for a moment. When it came to realistic combat, kickboxing was king. Nowhere else could a fighter throw full-power kicks and punches and, if Thai rules were used, elbows and knees.

When it came to cross-training, multiculturalism was it. Practitioners loved to tell people things like, "I do the Korean arts for kicking, the Japanese arts for punching, the Philippine arts for weapons and the Indonesian arts for close-range combat."

When it came to sheer, unadulterated toughness, the Sabaki Challenge and the Shidokan Open were on top. Their bone-breaking bare-knuckle bouts were the domain of karate's baddest dudes.

Then, in early 1993, Rorion Gracie and Art Davie hatched a plan for a new test of combat skills. Dubbed the Ultimate Fighting Championship, it would pit practitioners of a variety of martial arts against one another in a three-tiered tournament. The winner of the first event, held in late 1993, as well as the second event and a couple of big bouts afterward, was Royce. Single-handedly, he established the Gracie name in America and around the world. In doing so, he redefined realistic combat, cross-training and our concept of toughness.

Black Belt caught up with Royce, now 40, in between seminar tours and pelted him with questions about his family's style of jiu-jitsu, his life after the UFC and his role in changing the history of the martial arts.

—Editor

Black Belt: It's nearly 15 years after the Ultimate Fighting Championship began. In your view, how did your performance in its first few shows affect the martial arts world?

Royce Gracie: Now everybody knows *jiu-jitsu*. The same way that all the grapplers learned that they have to incorporate some type of stand-up martial arts like boxing or kickboxing—even if they don't use it—the stand-up guys learned that they have to incorporate some type of grappling. That grappling is usually Gracie jiu-jitsu. It was a big eye-opener for the martial arts world.

BB: When you began winning, the first reaction of many martial artists was denial. Then it seemed as though they relented and reluctantly studied jiu-jitsu. What about now? Are they still learning it because they have to, or are they actually eager to pick up ground skills?

Royce: When the UFC started, many people didn't even consider grappling a martial art. Many times since then, I've had grapplers come up to me and say, "Thanks for putting us on the map." Today, everyone wants to learn some type of grappling. If they cannot get their hands on Gracie jiu-jitsu, they settle for judo or wrestling or something along those lines.

They realize that grappling is important to know in case they go to the ground in a fight. If you can knock a guy out with one punch and the fight is over, perfect. That's a beautiful fight. But if the guy is bigger and

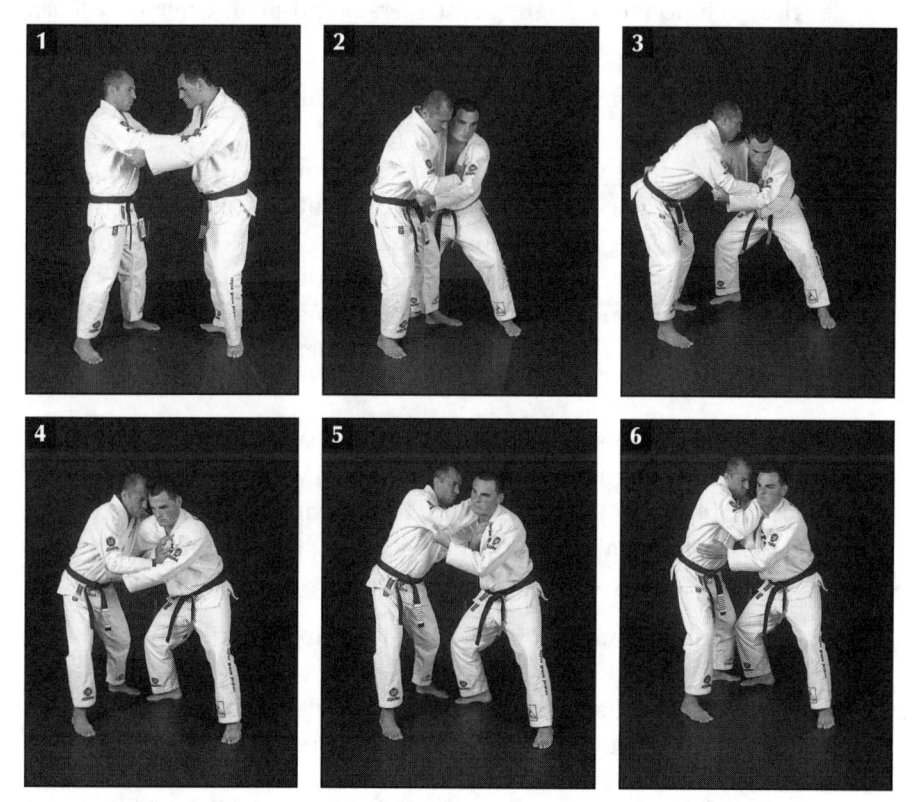

Royce Gracie (left) and Ralek Gracie tie up (1). Ralek attempts a hip throw (2), and Royce blocks by moving his hips backward and placing his left hand and forearm against his opponent's hip (3). Royce repositions his left foot and transfers the man's collar from his right hand to his left (4). He then slides his right hand along his neck and grabs the back of his collar with his thumb inside (5). To apply the choke, Royce pulls with his left arm and pushes with his right (6).

stronger and can absorb your punch, you've got to take him to the ground and choke him out. That's what we've always taught.

BB: How widespread is the popularity of Brazilian jiu-jitsu?

Royce: I do seminars around the world. The average number of people at each one is 40 to 50, which is a lot. I normally spend about 15 days at home with my family and 15 days on the road teaching, and I'm booked far in advance. Jiu-jitsu's popularity is definitely growing.

BB: Which group is your favorite to teach: military, police or civilians?

Royce: Civilians. You can see it in their eyes when they learn something new. They're like, Why didn't I think of that? Especially beginners—they really appreciate the techniques they're learning.

BB: These days, would it be fair to say that every mixed-martial arts fighter knows Brazilian jiu-jitsu?

Royce: Even if they don't do it, they know some of the techniques. Even people who do judo and wrestling learn Gracie jiu-jitsu. Once they learn it, they combine the moves with their own style.

BB: What about world-class wrestlers? Isn't their style of grappling enough for the ground portion of MMA fighting?

Royce: In wrestling, you don't have submissions. Wrestling is enough to take a guy down and control him, but then what do you do? Let the guy get back up and do it again and hope to win by points? What if you face a guy who offers some resistance and won't let you take him down? What if you get only one chance to take him down? Maybe you could finish it with a submission then and there. Jiu-jitsu is an excellent supplement for every style out there.

BB: If a fighter adopts Brazilian jiu-jitsu as his base, what skills would you recommend he augment it with for use in MMA?

Royce: Thai boxing. I'm a big fan of Thai boxing. I go to Fairtex quite a bit, and they help me a lot. It's the best striking style for MMA because it teaches elbows and knees. They also do takedowns such as the foot sweep.

BB: Is a combination of Brazilian jiu-jitsu and Thai boxing the best for self-defense, too?

Royce: Gracie jiu-jitsu is enough for self-defense. We cover escapes from every position that you can imagine. If you're talking about an MMA fight, however, it's a different story.

BB: How has your family's art changed over the past 15 years?

Royce: A perfect example comes from Ralek Gracie, my nephew. He

THE ULTIMATE GUIDE TO BRAZILIAN JIU-JITSU

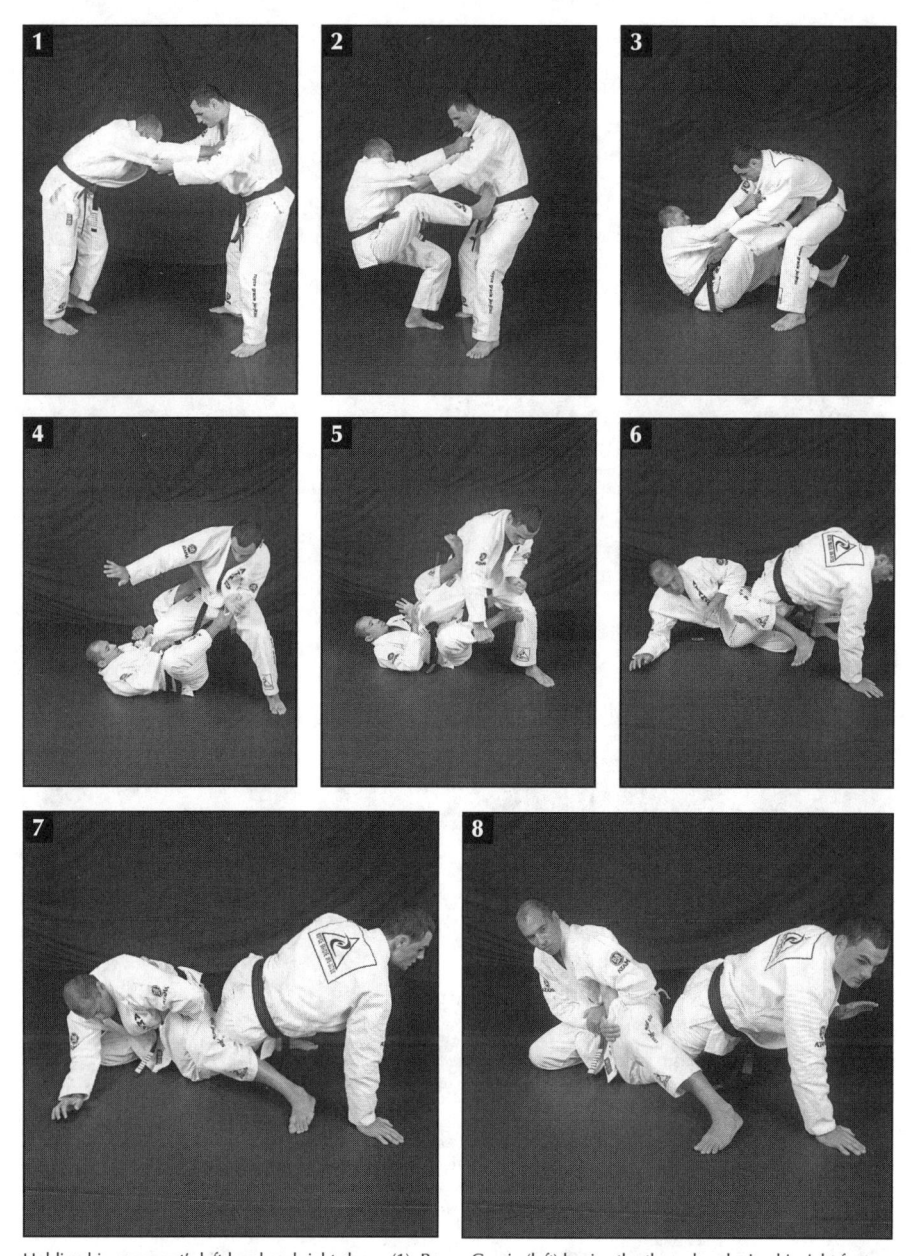

Holding his opponent's left lapel and right sleeve (1), Royce Gracie (left) begins the throw by placing his right foot on the man's stomach (2). Gracie sits and attempts to lean back, but the opponent resists (3). Gracie immediately grabs the man's right foot and pulls himself under him so he can wrap his left leg around his right thigh (4). Next, Gracie's right foot pushes against the man's left knee (5), toppling him (6). Gracie traps the ankle with his left arm (7), and after creating a figure-4 grip, applies a foot lock (8).

BLACK BELT

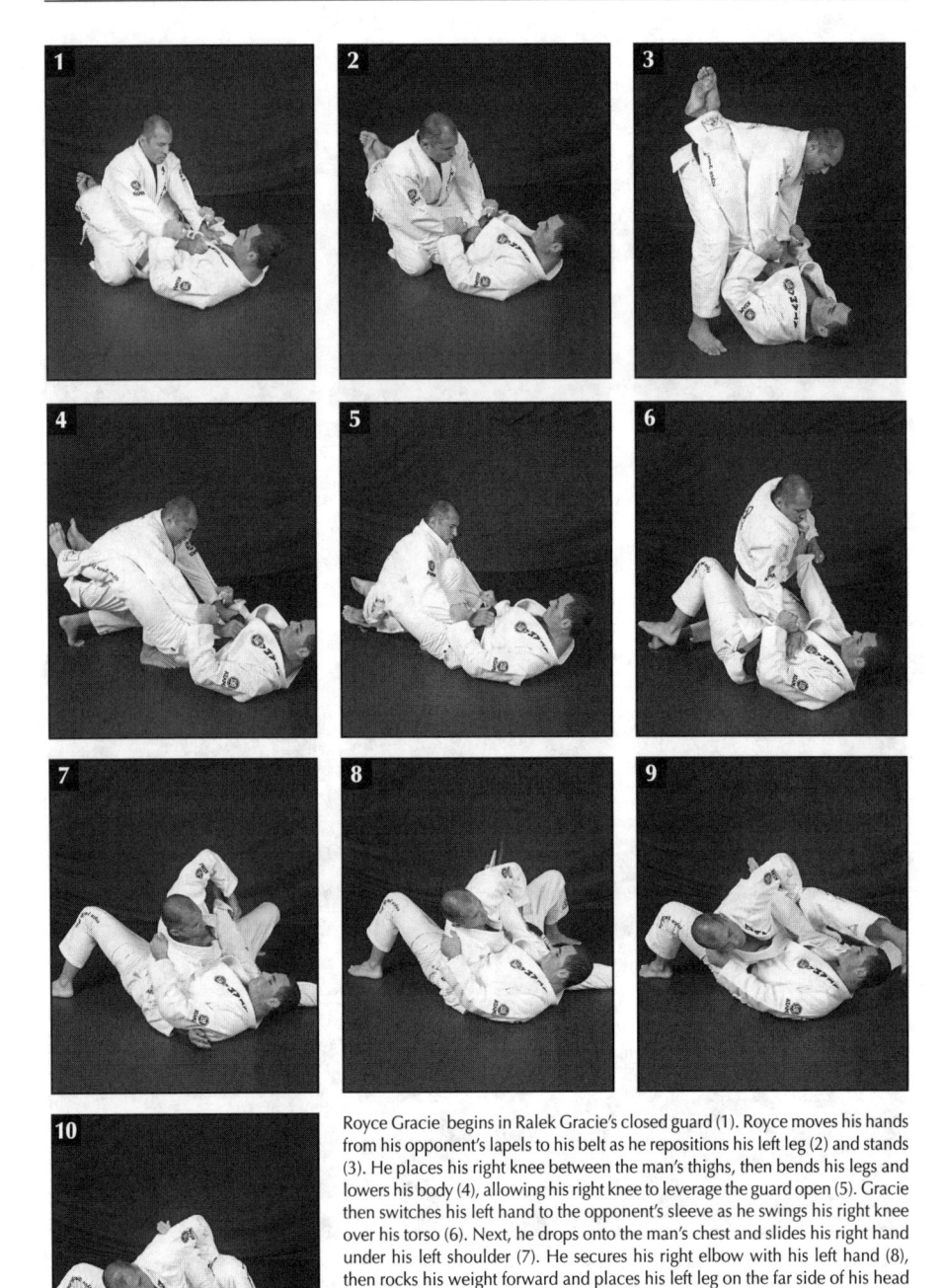

Royce Gracie begins in Ralek Gracie's closed guard (1). Royce moves his hands from his opponent's lapels to his belt as he repositions his left leg (2) and stands (3). He places his right knee between the man's thighs, then bends his legs and lowers his body (4), allowing his right knee to leverage the guard open (5). Gracie then switches his left hand to the opponent's sleeve as he swings his right knee over his torso (6). Next, he drops onto the man's chest and slides his right hand under his left shoulder (7). He secures his right elbow with his left hand (8), then rocks his weight forward and places his left leg on the far side of his head (9). To apply pressure on the trapped limb, he leans backward (10).

had a fight in K-1 HERO's in July 2007. He used a side kick, got in a clinch, took his opponent down and mounted him before going for the arm lock. I think he used a couple of hits to soften the guy up first. It was a classic fight even though it was from a kid who's 22 years old and part of a new generation of up-and-coming fighters. The basics of jiu-jitsu don't change. The strategy—how you approach the fight—might change, but the foundation of the house is the same.

BB: MMA competition has evolved away from the use of uniforms. When you teach these days, do you focus more on no-*gi* training?

Royce: No. Most of my seminars are with a gi. My law-enforcement seminars are no-gi, of course. I do a lot of gi training when I work out. If I'm preparing for a fight in America, I train no-gi because we're not allowed to wear a gi. But if I'm training just to train—to roll around—I prefer to wear a gi because you have more tools to play with. It's like boxing, in which you can use only your hands, versus *muay Thai*, in which you can use your hands, feet, elbows and knees. When you have more tools to use, it becomes more fun. No-gi fighting has a very limited number of chokes and locks.

BB: When you started competing in the UFC, Brazilian jiu-jitsu fighters could win with just the basics. But now, it seems as though it takes a higher level of technique to win. What's changed?

Royce: It's still classic jiu-jitsu. The difference is that some fighters are more aware of what's coming, so they hide their arms. When they do that, you have to go for a choke or a foot lock. You have to keep changing to find the opening, instead of just going for one technique and running the risk that they'll block it.

BB: Do you also try to create openings?

Royce: You have to do that, too. You cannot depend on them feeding you something. You've got to put a lot of things out there to get them to leave an opening.

BB: How good are the Brazilian jiu-jitsu skills we see in MMA nowadays? Are they high level, or are the fighters successful only because they're combining so-so jiu-jitsu with decent kickboxing skills?

Royce: The fighters are very skilled. Most of the ones from Brazil have won world championships. The problem is, there's no money in jiu-jitsu competition. They get to a certain point in their life and decide they need to make money. That's why they enter MMA.

BLACK BELT

BB: Who are the best American fighters out there now?

Royce: Randy Couture is definitely a tough cookie. I'm an old man, too, so he's my kind of guy. Chuck Liddell is also a great fighter. He's had a couple of tough matches and just has to put his head back in the game. There are lots of good guys—it's hard to name all of them.

BB: Which MMA athlete do you most like to watch? Who's the most entertaining?

Royce: The Chute Boxe guys. They either do the knockout or get knocked

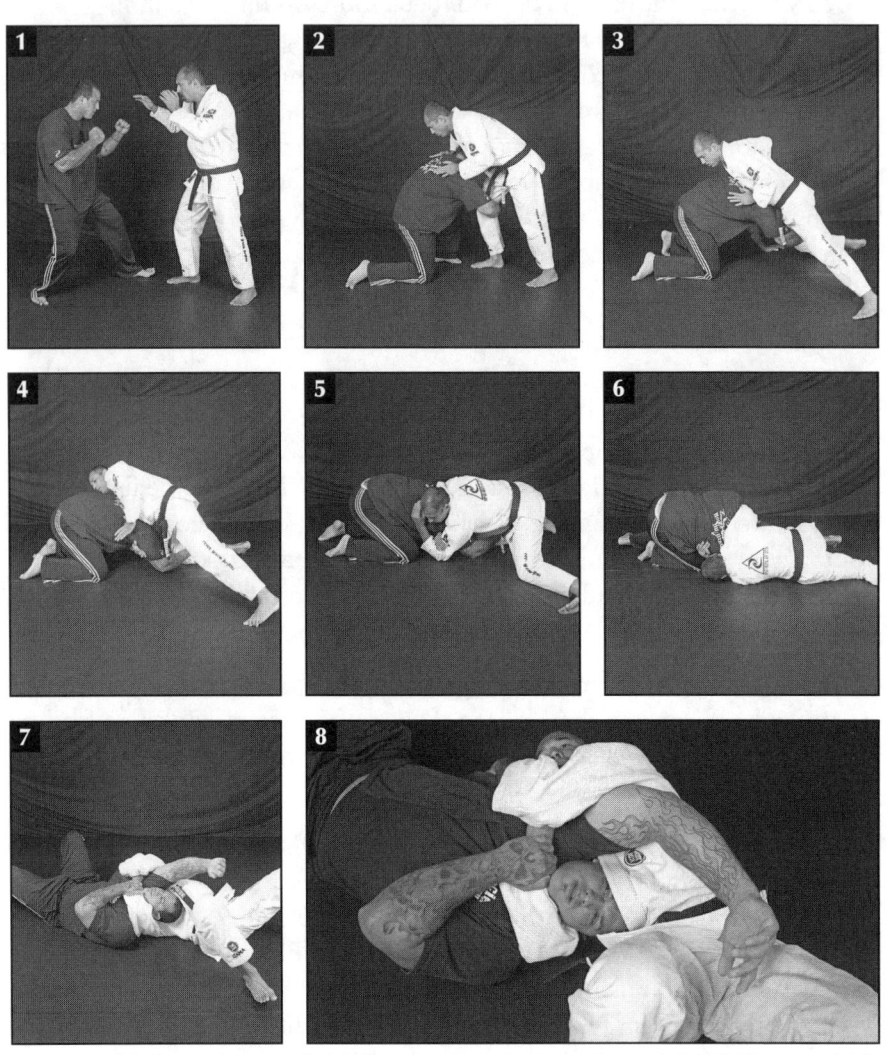

Alex Di Ciero (left) shoots in for a single-leg takedown (1-2). Royce Gracie sprawls (3) and slips his right arm around the man's neck (4). After locking his fingers on his left biceps, he places his left palm against the man's back (5). Gracie extends his left leg and rolls onto his left shoulder (6) and then his back (7). From there, he tightens his hold for the choke (8).

out. You never see a boring fight from them.

BB: Do you have any students who are rising through the MMA ranks?

Royce: Buddy Clinton. He fights for King of the Cage. He hasn't won a title yet, but after a couple of wins, he's ready for a shot at the title.

BB: Are the skills you teach students like Clinton the same as what you taught 15 years ago?

Royce: The foundation is the same. After you build the foundation, the student has to add his personal style.

BB: What are the most common mistakes you see as you conduct your seminars?

Royce: People trying to take shortcuts. Instead of going from one to two to three, sometimes they think, I want to go from one to three to make it faster. But when they do that, they lose the technique. I tell them to slow down. Speed comes with time. Strength you add later.

BB: Say a person wants to be an MMA fighter. What advice would you give him with respect to techniques, conditioning and strength?

Royce: First, to win a fight, you've got to know what you're doing. If you don't know what you're doing, you have no reason to be in the ring. Second, you can have the fastest or most powerful car in the world, but if it doesn't have gas, you're not going anyplace. You've got to fill up the tank—that's techniques. Then comes strength. So it goes in that order: You've got to know what you're doing and have the techniques, then develop the conditioning and strength.

BB: After that, is it a matter of gaining experience, of working your way up?

Royce: You can try to take a shortcut, but in the end, you've got to build a reputation. A lot of guys think, I'm not going to fight unless I get a shot at the title. But who the heck are they? They have to prove themselves before they get to fight the champ.

BB: How long should an aspiring fighter expect to compete before he makes money?

Royce: If a guy steps into the ring, he should get paid. But there's a ranking. If you build your way up and fight the top guys, you should get more money. If you fight no-names, you get paid less. That's the nature of the business.

BB: When is your next fight?

Royce: I'm getting too old for this. (laughs) Once a year is plenty for me. My next fight won't be until next year.

BB: When you're training for a fight, what's a typical week like?

Royce: Monday through Saturday, I do 45 minutes to an hour of stand-up—mostly *muay Thai*—and 45 minutes to an hour of grappling. I also lift weights three or four days a week. Conditioning I do 50 minutes to an hour three or four days a week. I might put a couple of runs in, no more than four miles, in the sand on the beach.

BB: What's the biggest project on the horizon for you?

Royce: Right now, I'm concentrating on teaching and conducting seminars. I'm very busy with that. My biggest project, though, is taking care of my family and raising my four kids.

UP CLOSE AND PERSONAL WITH KYRA GRACIE
Meet the Newest Star of the Legendary Brazilian Grappling Family!

Photos by Rick Hustead • Black Belt • June 2008

You could safely say that there's no martial artist in the West who hasn't heard the name "Gracie"—whether it's attached to Rickson, Royce, Rorion, Renzo, Ralph, Royler or Carlson; to one of Brazilian jiu-jitsu's patriarchs, Helio and Carlos Sr.; or to one of the up-and-coming fighters like Ralek and Ryon. Obviously, the family has left an indelible mark on the modern history of the martial arts. Noticeably absent from that list, however, is the name of even one woman. That's because, in the rough-and-tumble world of grappling, Gracie girls are practically nonexistent.

Enter Kyra Gracie, the woman who won the 132-pound division at the 2007 Abu Dhabi Combat Club Submission Wrestling World Championships. The Brazilian native is now based in Southern California, and she has big plans to increase the number of women participating in jiu-jitsu around the world. We expect to see a lot more of her in the future as her skills develop and her competition career continues, so we're offering the following as an introduction.

—*Editor*

Age: 22
Marital status: single
Place of birth: Rio de Janeiro, Brazil
Mother: Flavia Gracie
Famous uncles: Ralph Gracie, Renzo Gracie
Grandfather: Robson Gracie
Date of arrival in the United States: 2005
Place of residence: Irvine, California
Hobbies: *jiu-jitsu*, traveling, spending time at the beach
Dojo at which she teaches: "I don't teach regularly, but I do seminars on the weekends."
Rank: black belt
Date of promotion to black belt: 2006
Promoted by: Carlos Gracie Jr. of Gracie Barra
Current instructor: Carlos Gracie Jr. "But I also have the pleasure of training with other members of my family, such as Renzo and Rilion."
Years she won the Abu Dhabi Combat Club Submission Wrestling World Championships: 2005, 2007 "They just started having the ADDC for women in 2005."

Years she won the World Brazilian Jiu-Jitsu Championship: 2004, 2006

Years she won the Pan-American Brazilian Jiu-Jitsu Games: 2001, 2002, 2003, 2005, 2007

Next tournament on her agenda: World Brazilian Jiu-Jitsu Championship in June 2008

Favorite technique: *omo plata*

Favorite Brazilian jiu-jitsu competitor: Roger Gracie

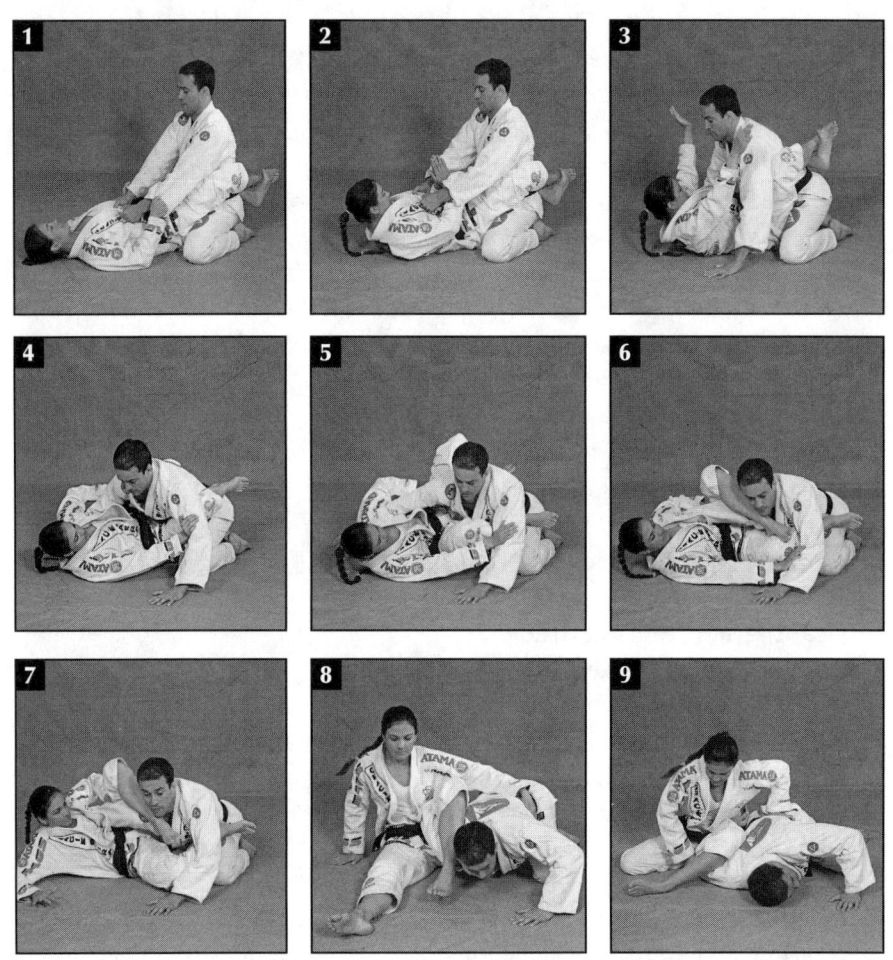

Omo Plata: Kyra Gracie begins with Marcio Feitosa in her closed guard (1). To break his grip on her lapels and make him post his arms, she spears her hands upward from underneath his forearms (2-3). She picks the arm she wants to attack—in this case, his right—and turns to her right as she pushes away his left arm (4). She traps his right arm in her armpit while placing her right foot on his left hip (5). Next, she swings her leg over Feitosa's limb and places her shin alongside his neck (6). Gracie sits up (7), wrenching the arm behind her opponent's back (8). Tapout pressure comes when she lifts her hips off the mat and, if necessary, pushes the trapped elbow down (9).

THE ULTIMATE GUIDE TO BRAZILIAN JIU-JITSU

Jumping Gogo Plata: Kyra Gracie faces her foe (1). As soon as he's within range, she goes airborne, grabbing the back of his neck (2) on her way to wrapping her legs around his torso and controlling his right arm (3). She moves her left foot to his hip and pulls his head down (4) so she can more easily place her left leg over his head (5). When her foot is in position against his throat, she grabs her toes and chokes (6). If additional pressure is needed, she can use her free hand to push on her heel (7).

Favorite Ultimate Fighting Championship fighter: Antonio Rodrigo "Minotauro" Nogueira

Prospects for ever fighting in a mixed-martial arts match: "Maybe yes, maybe no."

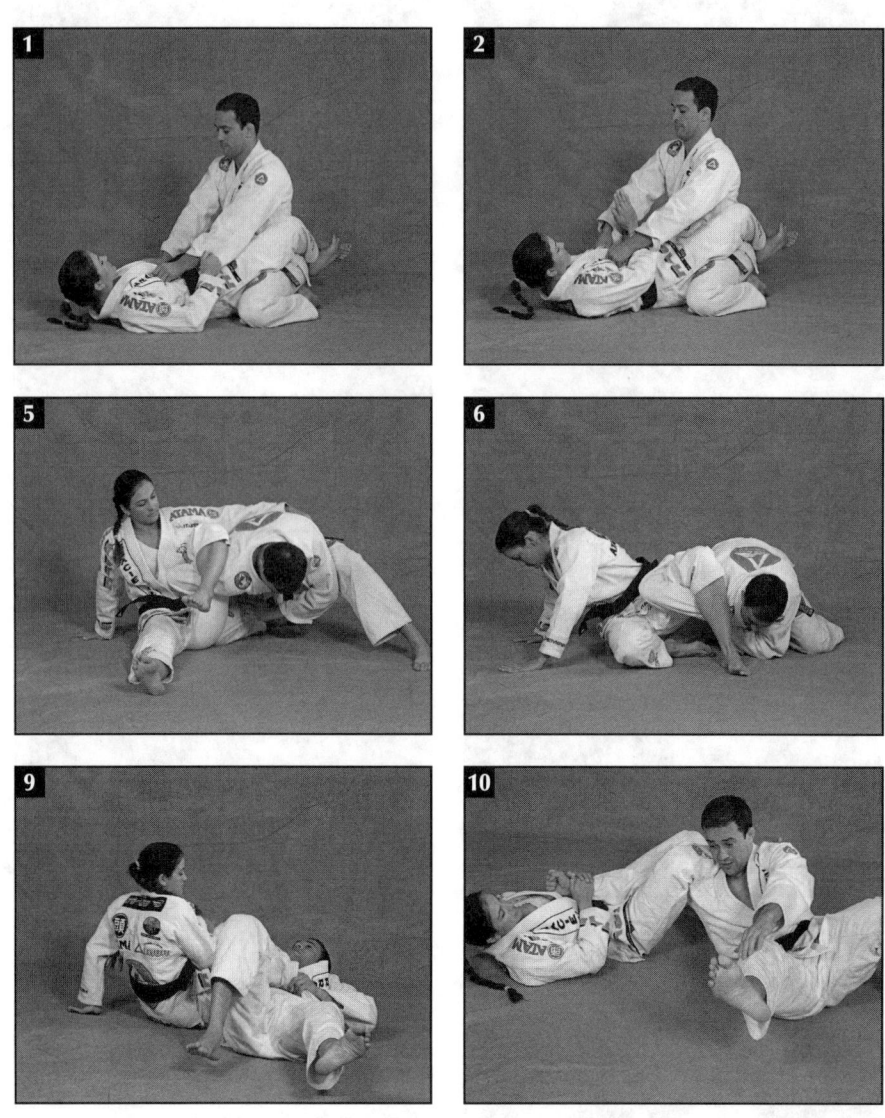

Omo Plata to Armbar: Kyra Gracie holds her opponent in her guard (1), then breaks his grip on her uniform (2-3) and shifts into position for the *omo plata* (4). He resists by locking his hands (5), which causes Gracie to rotate her hips around his upper arm to break his grip (6-7). She continues her rotary motion, flipping the man onto his back (8-9). Although she's holding his wrist, he manages to sit up before she can place her leg over his head (10). To regain control, she swings her left leg over his face (11) and executes an armbar (12).

Martial arts goal: "To get more women involved in Brazilian jiu-jitsu."

Family's reaction when she decided to compete: "In the beginning, it was tough because a lot of my family is old-fashioned and didn't think a girl should be doing this, but now they all support me."

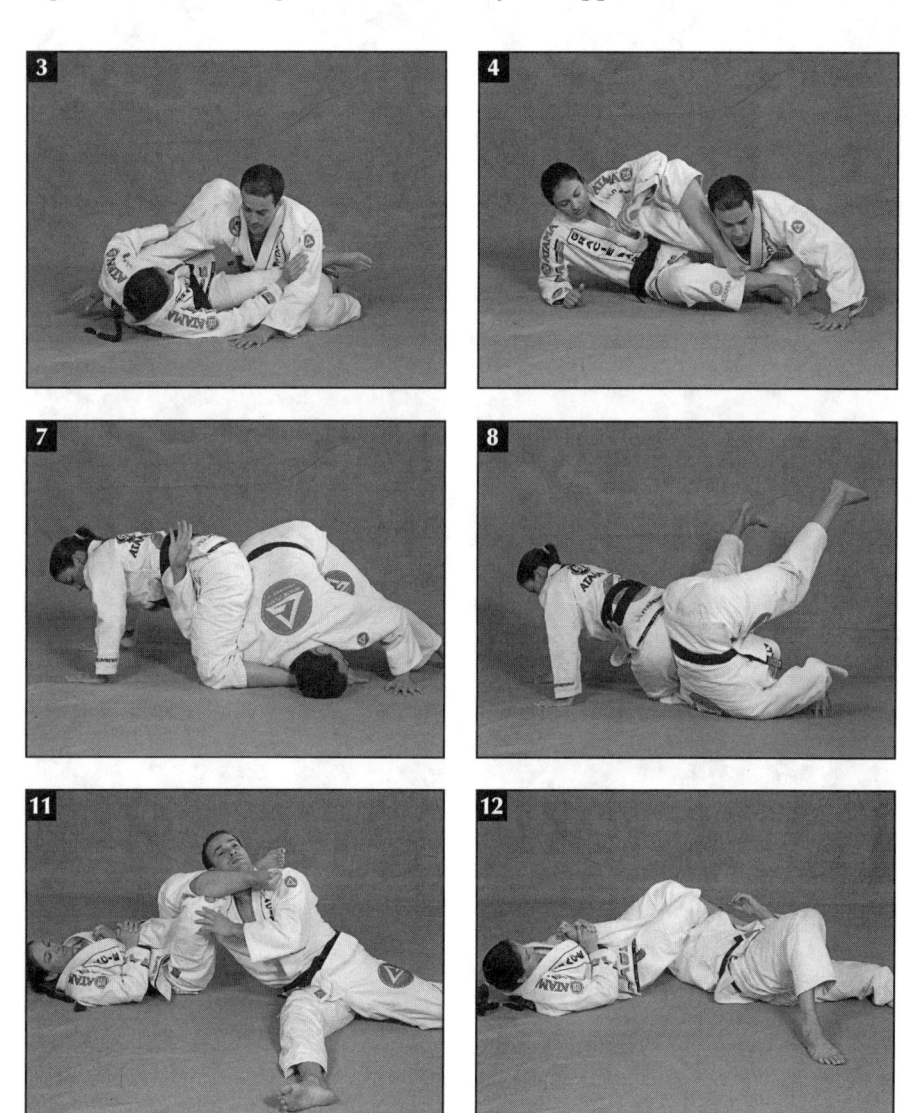

BLACK BELT

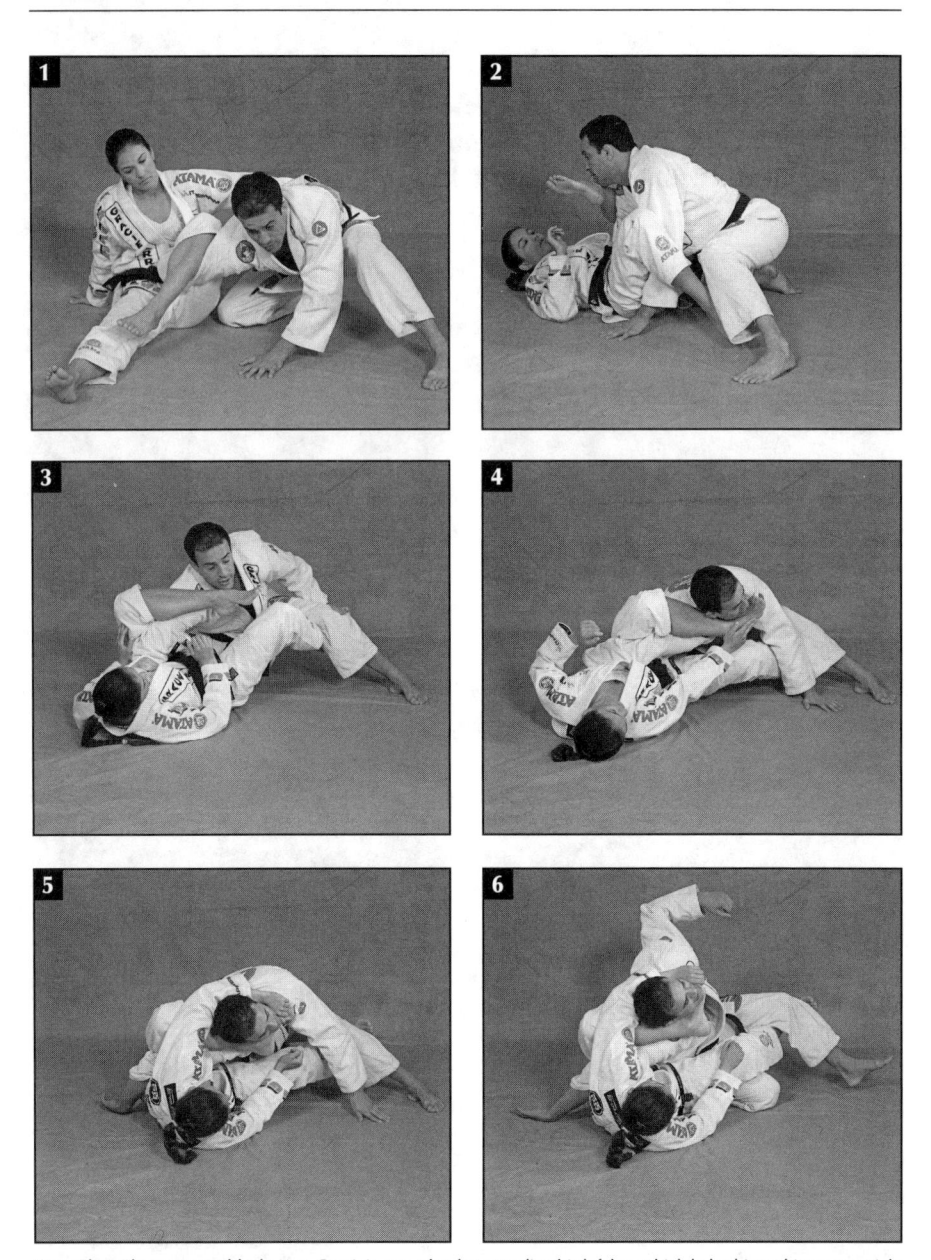

Gogo Plata: The opponent blocks Kyra Gracie's *omo plata* by extending his left leg, which helps him achieve an upright posture (1). He turns toward her and shifts his weight onto her body, causing her to fall backward (2). Gracie maneuvers her left leg over his right arm and hooks her right foot under his left leg (3). If necessary, she can use her hand to push her foot tight against the opponent's neck while extending her right leg to break his base (4). After that, she reaches around the back of his head and grabs her toes (5). To finish, she applies choking pressure with her arm and leg (6).

MORE from Black Belt Books

TRAINING FOR COMPETITION: Brazilian Jiu-Jitsu and Submission Grappling
by David Meyer

Brazilian *jiu-jitsu* champion and world champion coach David Meyer shares his knowledge of competition-winning strategies in *Training for Competition: Brazilian Jiu-Jitsu and Submission Grappling*. Drawing upon his 20-plus years of teaching, grappling and competition experience, Meyer helps novice and veteran grapplers alike enhance their overall technique, strengthen their physical condition, learn to take calculated risks, develop a game plan, use the points to their advantage, find a great coach, reduce stress and much more. With detailed photo sequences and added insights from grappling authorities like Bas Rutten, Cesar Gracie, Gene LeBell and Wally Jay, *Training for Competition* gives fighters their best chance at attaining victory! 191 pgs.
(ISBN-13: 978-0-89750-167-5)
Book Code 495—Retail $24.95

PHILOSOPHY OF FIGHTING: Morals and Motivations of the Modern Warrior
by Keith Vargo

The thoughtful writings of Keith Vargo, the popular author of *Black Belt's* Way of the Warrior column, are compiled in the *Philosophy of Fighting: Morals and Motivations of the Modern Warrior*. Comprising a decade's worth of discourses, the book entertains and provokes readers by examining the trends, traditions, cultures, fields and thinkers that shape the martial arts with the watchful eye of a psychologist. By exploring philosophical questions, *Philosophy of Fighting* encourages readers to actively consider the key elements that define the modern warrior in a contemporary world. 231 pgs.
(ISBN-13: 978-0-89750-174-3)
Book Code 500—Retail $16.95

To order, call (800) 581-5222 or visit www.blackbeltmag.com/shop

MORE from Black Belt Books

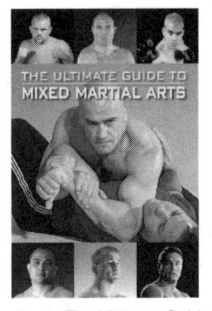

THE ULTIMATE GUIDE TO MIXED MARTIAL ARTS
by the Editors of Black Belt

Only one sport has reinforced elbow smashes to the head, flying knees and liver kicks. From MMA's controversial inception to its mainstream acceptance, from the iconic legacy of Rickson Gracie to the freakish knockout power of Chuck Liddell, from the unstoppable determination of Randy Couture to the emergence of tomorrow's champions, *Black Belt* has covered the sport's genesis and evolution. With *The Ultimate Guide to Mixed Martial Arts*, you will leap into the octagon with Chuck Liddell, experience the artery-crushing chokes of Rickson Gracie, devour Randy Couture's prescription for peak performance, master Dan Henderson's winning training methods and suffer the nasty takedowns of UFC bad-boy Tito Ortiz. A compilation of instructional articles and interviews with the industry's greatest champions, *The Ultimate Guide to Mixed Martial Arts* is the definitive resource on the athletes and techniques of the world's most intense and popular new sport. 216 pgs. (ISBN-13: 978-0-89750-159-0) **Book Code 488—Retail $16.95**

THE ULTIMATE GUIDE TO GRAPPLING
by the Editors of Black Belt

Attention, grapplers! This is the book you've been waiting for. From the arenas of ancient Rome to the mixed-martial arts cages of modern Las Vegas, men have always wrestled for dominance. Ground fighting is the cornerstone of combat, and *The Ultimate Guide to Grappling* pays homage to the art with three decades' worth of instructional essays and interviews collected from the archives of *Black Belt*. With more than 30 articles featuring legends like Mike Swain, John Machado, Gokor Chivichyan, Hayward Nishioka, Renzo Gracie, Bart Vale and B.J. Penn, you'll learn the legacy of Greek *pankration*, reality-based ground techniques for police officers and soldiers, the differences between classical *jujutsu* and submission wrestling and more! Transform your traditional art into a well-rounded and effective self-defense system today! 232 pgs. (ISBN-13: 978-0-89750-160-6) **Book Code 489—Retail $16.95**

THE ULTIMATE GUIDE TO STRIKING
by the Editors of Black Belt

The Ultimate Guide to Striking examines striking techniques from various martial arts. Topics include *jeet kune do's* most efficient weapons, modern applications of *isshin-ryu* karate, vital-point attacks for women's self-defense, the vicious spinning backfist of *The Ultimate Fighter's* Shonie Carter, the "combat slap," *tang soo do's* lethal elbow strikes, the mysterious art of *mi zong* kung fu, Jeff Speakman's rapid-fire *kenpo* arsenal and more! Through scores of detailed photos and articles printed in *Black Belt* from 1990 to 2005, *The Ultimate Guide to Striking* provides a vast cultural and technical cross-section on the topic of striking. This collection is sure to be an enlightening and effective addition to any martial artist's training library. 248 pgs. (ISBN-13: 978-0-89750-154-5) **Book Code 483—Retail $16.95**

THE ULTIMATE GUIDE TO KNIFE COMBAT
by the Editors of Black Belt

More effective than a fist and more accessible than a gun, the knife is the most pragmatic self-defense tool. *The Ultimate Guide to Knife Combat* celebrates this simple, versatile, sometimes controversial weapon with essays and instructional articles written by the world's foremost experts, including Ernest Emerson, Hank Hayes, Jim Wagner and David E. Steele. *The Ultimate Guide to Knife Combat* presents an international cross-section of knife cultures and styles—from the heroic legacy of America's bowie knife to the lethal techniques of the *kukri*-wielding Gurkhas of Nepal—and features essential empty-hand techniques, exercises to improve your fighting skills, and advice on choosing the knife that's right for you. Spanning two decades of material from the *Black Belt* archives, *The Ultimate Guide to Knife Combat* provides everything you need to know about fighting with or against a blade. 312 pgs. (ISBN-13: 978-0-89750-158-3) **Book Code 487—Retail $16.95**

To order, call (800) 581-5222 or visit www.blackbeltmag.com/shop

MORE from Black Belt Books

GRACIE JIU-JITSU: The Master Text
by Helio Gracie
This 8-1/2" x 11" 284-page hard-bound full color masterpiece is packed with more than 1,300 photos! This collector-quality first edition will be one of the most sought-after books in the martial arts world for years to come. Be one of the few to own the first edition of *Gracie Jiu-Jitsu: The Master Text*. In a clear and easy-to-follow format, Helio Gracie addresses different aspects of the Brazilian *jiu-jitsu* method that bears his name. From the first page to the last, you'll get a simple break down of how to systematically progress and technically improve your mat game regardless of your background or grappling ability. Now older than 90 and still training and teaching, Gracie has left an enduring worldwide legacy that can only be found in *Gracie Jiu-Jitsu: The Master Text*. (ISBN-13: 978-0-9759411-1-9)
Book Code 902—Retail $70

BRAZILIAN JUJUTSU: Side-Mount Techniques
by Joe Moreira with Daniel Darrow 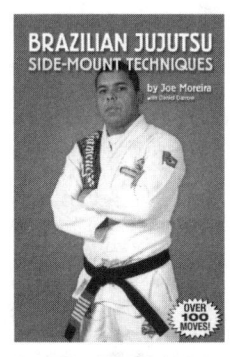
Describing more than 100 moves through photographic sequences and detailed captions, Brazilian-*jujutsu* fighter Joe Moreira uses his "sequential teaching" style to delineate the network of options available to combatants dealing with side-mount situations. Having trained with the likes of Reylson Gracie and Francisco Mansour in his homeland of Brazil, Moreira founded the United States Federation of Brazilian Jiu-Jitsu and 30 branches of the Joe Moreira Jiu-Jitsu de Brazil across the United States. Today, Moreira continues to be involved with events such as the Ultimate Fighting Championship and instructs mixed martial artists such as Kimo Leopoldo. Whether you are a student, teacher or simply a fan of jujutsu, this edition will serve as a comprehensive reference for side-mount moves and will instill a deeper understanding of the art's emphasis on technique rather than strength. 149 pgs. (ISBN-13: 978-0-89750-145-3) **Book Code 475—Retail $12.95**

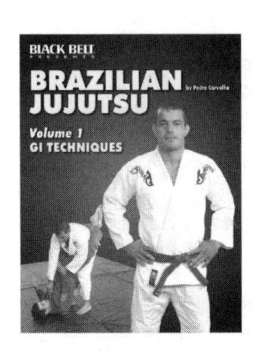

BRAZILIAN JUJUTSU VOLUME 1: Gi Techniques
by Pedro Carvalho
In *Volume 1*, Pedro Carvalho provides a strong technical foundation for the traditional *jujutsu* competitor by demonstrating techniques and submissions that utilize the *gi* (uniform). Topics include takedowns, passing the guard, finishing holds, north-south positioning, chokes, sweeps and attacks from the side, armbars and more. 80 pgs. Size: 8-1/2" x 11" (ISBN-13: 978-0-89750-150-7)
Book Code 480—Retail $13.95

BRAZILIAN JUJUTSU VOLUME 2: No-Gi Techniques
by Pedro Carvalho 
In *Volume 2*, Carvalho addresses the rising popularity of no-*gi jujutsu* (also called "submission wrestling")—a challenging and fast-paced style in which competitors forgo the gi and generally wear shorts and T-shirts. Topics include takedowns, guard passes, striking and mounting from the cross-body position, takedown counters, guard attacks, sweeps, escapes, rear-mount attacks and more. 78 pgs. Size: 8-1/2" x 11" (ISBN-13: 978-0-89750-151-4)
Book Code 481—Retail $13.95

To order, call (800) 581-5222 or visit www.blackbeltmag.com/shop

MORE from Black Belt Books

ADVANCED JUJITSU:
The Science Behind the Gentle Art
by George Kirby

Transcending the mere memorization of *kata*, forms and techniques, George Kirby takes you into advanced concepts that will simplify your training, help you learn new techniques faster and grant you deeper access to the inner workings of *jujitsu*. These concepts can be applied to the entire spectrum of martial arts because they address the fundamentals of technique, physics, anatomy, relaxation, humility, self-confidence and open-mindedness. 131 pgs.
(ISBN-13: 978-0-89750-152-1) **Book Code 482—Retail $16.95**

JUJITSU NERVE TECHNIQUES:
The Invisible Weapon of Self-Defense
by George Kirby

George Kirby analyzes and charts the human body's multitude of nerve and pressure points—and then presents submission techniques that utilize pain induction to bring an attacker under control without injury! A fascinating study of the human body as both a weapon and target, with extensive photo sequences, detailed technique breakdowns, and nerve- and pressure-point charts. 236 pgs.
(ISBN-13: 978-0-89750-142-2) **Book Code 473—Retail $16.95**

JUJITSU:
Basic Techniques of the Gentle Art
by George Kirby

This fully illustrated book includes an explanation of *ki* (internal energy) and use of momentum, joint locks, throws, pressure points and nerve attacks. George Kirby is chairman of the American Jujitsu Association.
128 pgs. (ISBN-13: 978-0-89750-088-3)
Book Code 425—Retail $9.95

JUJITSU:
Intermediate Techniques of the Gentle Art
by George Kirby

Following his first book, which covered basic *jujitsu* skills, George Kirby presents the intermediate techniques. Fully illustrated. 256 pgs.
(ISBN-13: 978-0-89750-128- 6)
Book Code 441—Retail $18.95

To order, call (800) 581-5222 or visit www.blackbeltmag.com/shop

MORE from Black Belt Books

BRUCE LEE'S FIGHTING METHOD: The Complete Edition
by Bruce Lee and M. Uyehara

Bruce Lee's Fighting Method: The Complete Edition brings the iconic four-volume *Fighting Method* series together into one definitive book. Intended as an instructional document to complement Lee's foundational *Tao of Jeet Kune Do*, this restored and enhanced edition of *Fighting Method* breathes new life into hallowed pages with digitally remastered photography and a painstakingly refurbished interior design for improved instructional clarity. This 492-page hard-bound book also includes 900-plus digitally enhanced images, newly discovered photographs from Lee's personal files, a new chapter on the Five Ways of Attack penned by famed first-generation student Ted Wong, and an analytical introduction by Shannon Lee that helps readers contextualize the revisions and upgrades implemented for this special presentation of her father's work. 492 pgs.
Size 7" x 10". (ISBN-13: 978-0-89750-170-5)
Book Code 494—Retail $34.95

CHINESE GUNG FU: The Philosophical Art of Self-Defense (Revised and Updated)
by Bruce Lee

Black Belt Books' new edition of *Chinese Gung Fu: The Philosophical Art of Self-Defense* gives martial arts enthusiasts and collectors exactly what they want: more Bruce Lee. In addition to the master's insightful explanations on *gung fu*, this sleek book features digitally enhanced photography, previously unpublished pictures with Lee's original handwritten notes, a brand-new front and back cover, and introductions by widow Linda Lee Cadwell and daughter Shannon Lee. Fully illustrated. 112 pgs. (ISBN-13: 978-0-89750-112-5)
Book Code 451—Retail $12.95

To order, call (800) 581-5222 or visit www.blackbeltmag.com/shop